ENSNARED
IN THE
WOLF'S
LAIR

Inside the **1944 PLOT** to Kill **HITLER** and the
GHOST CHILDREN of His **REVENGE**

ANN BAUSUM

NATIONAL
GEOGRAPHIC

Washington, D.C.

For all whose lives have been
forever touched by family separations

And for Sam
who enriched my world and this book
by sharing in its journeys

Contents

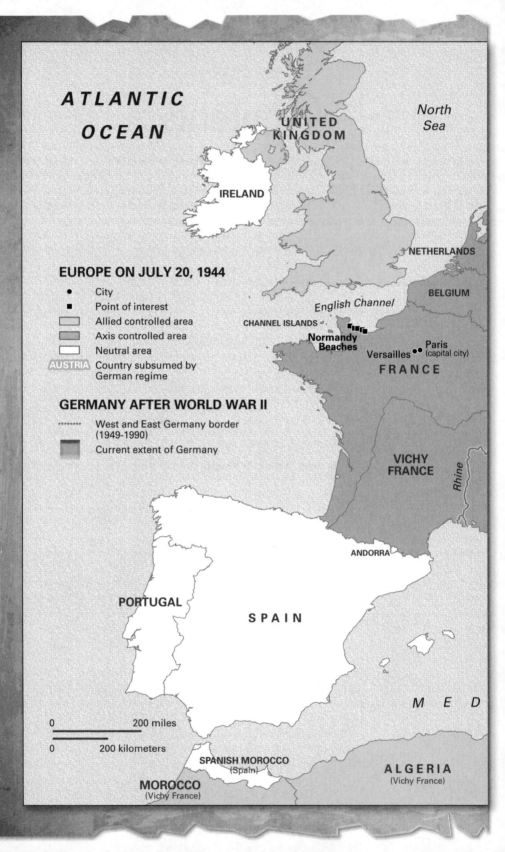

"It is now time for something to be done. But he who has the courage to do something must do so in the knowledge that he will go down in German history as a traitor. If he does not do it, however, then he will be a traitor to his own conscience."

Claus Schenk Graf von Stauffenberg
speaking to his wife, Nina,
ahead of the July 1944 coup attempt

Claus Schenk Graf von Stauffenberg, circa 1941

Introduction

"I'm finally getting optimistic," Anne Frank wrote in her diary on July 21, 1944. "Now, at last, things are going well! They really are!"

Hidden away in a secret apartment in the Netherlands, the Frank family and their fellow residents had heard the same news as the rest of the world. "An assassination attempt has been made on Hitler's life," the 15-year-old wrote. Eleven days passed before she returned to her diary once more. Then the entries stopped. Someone had betrayed the Franks and the other residents in their hidden apartment. On August 4 they became prisoners of the Nazi state.

Later that month a 12-year-old German girl named Christa von Hofacker picked up her pen and began to write in her own diary. She knew nothing about the Frank family. Nor was she aware of the Nazi Holocaust that would kill Frank and most of her family members along with 10 million others during World War II. Christa simply wanted to record her own wartime experiences.

As Anne Frank had done, she wrote partly to try to make sense of a world that had been blown apart during the regime of Adolf Hitler. In Christa's case a literal explosion had upended her life. Weeks earlier a bombing at Hitler's Wolfsschanze—his Wolf's Lair command post—had caused her respected father to be branded a traitor by association. Then he had vanished into the Nazi criminal court apparatus. Was he dead? Was he being tortured? Christa didn't know.

And so she wrote to confide her fears.

Within days Gestapo agents had come to her home and taken away her mother, older brother, and older sister. Supervision of Christa and her younger brother and sister had fallen to strangers assigned to live with them by the Nazis.

Then the Gestapo agents returned. They demanded that Christa and the younger children immediately gather a few belongings. The three of them had to leave home too. Accompanied by these guards, the siblings would embark on a trip to an unknown destination for inexplicable reasons with no indication of when—or if—they would ever return. When Christa packed, she added her diary to her suitcase. And after she and her siblings arrived, she wrote about what happened next. When the war ended in 1945, Christa had survived.

So had her diary.

Years later an edited version of it became celebrated in Germany as an eyewitness portrayal of a small but telling chapter in the history of the Nazi regime. Her story wasn't about the country's military defeat, and it didn't intersect with the Holocaust. Instead, her account reminded readers that there had been steadfast German resistance to the regime. It also served as a testament to Hitler's paranoia and to his determination to punish anyone who dared to challenge his authority. It showed that he relished using his enemies' family members as pawns, even if it meant separating children from their parents. In fact, so much the better if it meant separating children from their parents.

Seven decades later I read Christa's diary. And then we talked. Christa, of course, is no longer a child. She is an octogenarian living in California, a mother and grandmother, an avid gardener, enduringly youthful, still climbing mountains and hiking beside the sea. I met or spoke with other survivors of this history, too, both in the United States and in Germany. During a pair of trips abroad, I visited places that had been imprinted with their experiences.

The result is this book. Here is Christa's story and the stories of other Germans who were ensnared in the lair of the Nazi regime as it tumbled toward its demise.

But first there was Hitler's rise.

Members of Adolf Hitler's SS security forces gather for a Nazi Party conference in Nuremberg, Germany, September 1936.

CHAPTER 1

Hitler's Rise

"Words can be like tiny doses of arsenic: they are
swallowed unnoticed, appear to have no effect,
and then after a little time the toxic reaction sets in after all."

Victor Klemperer
The Language of the Third Reich, 1947

Word by word, dose by dose, his language charmed the people until there could be no other leader, no other führer.

After the First World War, Adolf Hitler seemed to say all the right things: Germans had been betrayed. Their government leaders had meekly accepted punishing terms of surrender in 1919. They had allowed the victors to seize territory that by rights belonged to the German people. They had impoverished the country by agreeing to pay massive fines for waging the war. And, in a final shocking concession, they had surrendered the right to rebuild the nation's military forces. Germany had been humiliated, great and noble Germany, he said.

Germans had other enemies, too, Hitler warned, especially Jews. By singling out members of the Jewish community, he exploited an ancient prejudice against a long-standing minority population in Europe. Many people shared his belief that Jews weren't really Germans. For how could they be when they were tied by their ancestry and faith to ancient Judaea? Never mind that Jewish people had made the continent their home for a millennium. Many fellow residents refused to accept them as Europeans; they were Jews and only Jews. Members of this religious group were cast as permanent outsiders, always "the other." And for a millennium that meant that Jews were blamed for any number of European calamities, from successive waves of plague to the hardships of the Great Depression.

When that financial calamity struck in 1929, it helped propel Hitler and his Nazi Party into power. Prior to this collapse of the world economy Nazis were only one of many smaller parties competing to gain influence in the country's 10-year-old government. But because Jews had traditionally been involved in finance and trade, Hitler was able to use the economic disaster to promote his party's anti-Semitic message.

Hitler spoke passionately and without regard for the truth. He claimed that Germany had been robbed by a conniving network of bankers and merchants. As he saw it, Jews were responsible for everyone else's suffering. Scarcity of supplies. Rising costs. Lack of work. Poverty. Look no further than the Jews, he insisted. Money was all they cared about. Not Germans. Not Germany. They were enemies of the people, said Hitler. But he and the Nazis were different. They cared only for true Germans and their nation.

Hitler's message stoked the flames of popular unrest by igniting the public's anger, and bitterness, and fear. He manipulated the facts or ignored them all together. He wove words into a seductive narrative that spoke to the increasing hardships in the country. The era's challenging circumstances gave credence to his poisonous speeches, and as time passed he found an increasingly receptive audience.

Word by word, dose by dose, he connected with people on an emotional level that made it easy for them to dismiss logical counterarguments. His message provoked resentment and discord in that way that can and has throughout history led rational people to lose all sense of reason—from building fires for burning so-called witches to holding picnics at mob-rule lynchings. Or believing the lies of a rising fascist dictator.

It didn't matter if opposing views were voiced by the news media, or intellectuals, or clergy members, or political foes. Hitler's message was simple, and it was compelling: *You've been wronged, and I can make things right.*

Like all false narratives, this one held enough fragments of truth to make it easy to swallow. People did feel wronged. They had been suffering. Their nation had been excessively penalized after the war. Their armed forces had shrunk to near oblivion. Their system of imperial rule had been dismantled in the wake of its defeat and replaced with an untested experiment in democracy. And then the world economy had

Signs in German and English warn residents to avoid buying goods from Jewish-owned stores, Berlin, April 1, 1933. Nazi Party security forces stood watch to discourage shopping during the daylong nationwide action.

collapsed. Germany had become a mess. So many factions competed for power that nothing got done. No one could agree on how to revive the country or what steps should be taken to help its citizens.

The voice of Adolf Hitler broke through that noise.

Having earned less than 3 percent of the national popular vote in 1928, the Nazi Party won 18 percent in 1930, one year after the stock market crash that triggered the Great Depression. When elections were held on July 31, 1932, a Catholic journalist named Fritz Gerlich warned Germans to turn away from Hitler when they went to the polls. Under a headline that characterized Nazism as a plague, he declared: "Adolf Hitler is preaching the legitimacy of lying. It is time for those of you who have fallen for the swindle of this power-mad individual to wake up!"

But few people heeded his warnings or those of the regime's other courageous critics. Nazi candidates won 37 percent of the vote, making theirs the most popular party in the highly fractured returns. The Nazi Party lost some ground during elections held later that year, but Hitler still retained considerable influence. And he used it.

Hitler leveraged his standing to expand his role in Germany's parliamentary government. Under this system, voters elected members of the national legislature and the country's president, but much of the power rested with the government's cabinet. It was the president's job to appoint these department heads and the chancellor who directed them. By early 1933 so much chaos and discontent pulsed through the government that it became hard to establish consistent leadership. In an attempt to stabilize the cabinet, the German president appointed Hitler to serve as chancellor on January 30, 1933. With this newfound authority, Hitler was able to exploit the volatile situation and manipulate the aging president, Paul von Hindenburg, into granting him additional powers.

"Some kind of fog has descended which is enveloping everybody," observed a German university professor named Victor Klemperer later that year. He watched the population around him being coerced, convinced, deceived, or otherwise led to support an immoral and criminal regime. The alchemy for that fog blended the same tools that Hitler had employed all along. The power of his personality. The power of propaganda. And the power of fear. Hitler's stirring speeches and the epic pageantry of Nazi Party events had turned him into a cultlike figure, a sort of demigod with an irresistible promise. He would restore Germany's prominence through what he called its Third Reich, or third age of greatness.

A Nazi propaganda poster declares, "Führer, we're following you!" Berlin, August 1934. The poster supported Hitler's consolidation of power after the death of the country's president.

It took until August 2, 1934, when the country's president died, for Hitler to complete his takeover of the German government. During his party's rise to power in 1932, he had failed to win the presidency outright. Hindenburg had been reelected instead. But, by the time of Hindenburg's death, Hitler had maneuvered to gain the authority to merge the duties of president with his role as chancellor. With Hindenburg gone and the office eliminated, there would be no further need for presidential elections. His conquest of the government was complete. Adolf Hitler had become the dictator of Germany, its führer.

Several key aides assured the longevity of Nazi rule, starting with loyal deputies Hermann Göring and Rudolf Hess. Another steadfast aide, Joseph Goebbels, controlled the regime's messaging through a department known as the Reich Ministry of Public Enlightenment and Propaganda. Goebbels dictated precisely what the public should hear about the country's affairs, truthful or otherwise. He shut down critical newspapers and made it clear that journalists who questioned the government were at risk of being jailed—or worse. Heinrich Himmler, who headed the Nazi's independent security staff, acted as the regime's enforcer. He took charge when critics needed to be silenced with imprisonment or intimidated with ruthless brutality.

Thus the regime sat poised like a perfectly balanced scale: On one side, terror. On the other, lies. And master over all, Adolf Hitler.

Hitler relied on the use of physical force to build and maintain his power. Early support had come from paramilitary gangs called Brownshirts, having been named for their uniform clothing. These forces became consolidated into a broader organization known by its signature initials, the SA. Its members did everything from committing acts of vandalism and violence against Jewish people to intimidating voters during key elections in 1932 and early 1933. A parallel group, referred to by its SS abbreviation, began as Hitler's personal security squad but grew to become a sort of private army. The Gestapo was a secret state police force that served as another tool for maintaining control.

While Hitler was consolidating his political power during 1933 and 1934, he also unified his authority over these groups. At the end of June 1934 he directed a purge of the SA leadership. He disliked the ambitions of its head, Ernst Röhm, and

Soldiers in the German armed forces swear their allegiance to Adolf Hitler, August 2, 1934.

wanted him killed. Hitler supervised the deadly operation himself, and it unfolded with such breathtaking cruelty that it became known as the Night of the Long Knives. Far more people died than Röhm. The regime admitted to 85 deaths, but closer to 200 people were killed.

Under Hitler's orders members of the SS executed political opponents and other enemies from across the country. Among those murdered was Fritz Gerlich, the journalist who had implored voters to wake up and recognize the Nazi plague. By the time of his death he had spent more than a year as a political prisoner at the regime's first concentration camp, Dachau.

Few objected to this chilling evidence of Hitler's brutal system of leadership. And why would they? Most residents accepted the explanation that those killed were a threat to the government. Many Germans had become fearful of the swaggering members of the SA and were undoubtedly glad to see the organization attacked. They also were mindful of the power of the regime itself. They understood that those who challenged it put not only themselves but innocent family members at risk of arrest or attack.

Most of all, Germans supported Hitler because their individual lives were beginning to improve. The worst effects of the Great Depression were fading; there were more opportunities for employment and fewer shortages in the marketplace. Political infighting and gridlock had ended with the establishment of the Nazi regime. Other nations treated Hitler's government as legitimate, so why should Germans question it? And even if someone disagreed with his policies, what leverage did one person have against an authoritative regime?

Hitler enjoyed widespread approval within the nation's armed forces. Its leadership supported his plan to defy the punitive postwar treaty and rebuild the German military. And they were relieved to see the SA lose power and influence. After Hitler's bloody summer massacre and his rise to absolute power, Germany's defense minister imposed a new oath of allegiance on members of the armed services. The change made sense to any commander trying to secure his position within the new regime. And the new oath may have carried a reassuring familiarity for military officers and soldiers. Until Germany's World War I defeat, all of them had sworn loyalty to the head of the imperial family, the kaiser. But their postwar promise had been to the country's new constitution. Swearing allegiance to one man may have felt like the return of a comforting tradition, even when that person was a civilian named Adolf Hitler.

And so they did.

This switch would impact the remaining history of the regime. Nothing strengthens a dictator like the loyalty of his nation's armed forces. And nothing breeds loyalty like the promise of "unconditional obedience" by someone who is trained to follow orders, especially when those orders are reinforced by a pledge "to risk my life at any time for this oath."

●·············●·············●·············●·············●

Among those newly sworn to obey the dictator was a promising young officer named Claus Schenk Graf von Stauffenberg. Democracy seemed like an unpredictable experiment to this talented cavalryman. He could appreciate aspects of the nation's enthusiasm for Hitler because he, too, supported such key Nazi principles as the value of a larger military, an economy based on hard work, a fight against corruption, and respect for living close to the land. Many of his fellow officers agreed and were, like him, following family customs by serving in uniform. Their names still carried hereditary titles such as Count *(Graf)* or Baron *(Freiherr)*. They were steeped in the heritage of imperial rule and the tradition of loyal service.

In July 1934, the month after the bloody Night of the Long Knives purge, Count von Stauffenberg became a father. He

Three generations of the von Stauffenberg family, Lautlingen, Germany, undated. The gathering included Claus (seated, second from right, with son Franz-Ludwig), his wife, Nina (in white), his mother, Caroline (standing), and his older brother Alexander (seated, left, holding Claus's son Berthold).

and his wife, Nina, named their firstborn after one of Claus's older twin brothers, Berthold. Two years later young Berthold and his parents moved with his baby brother to Germany's capital, Berlin. The couple relocated so that Claus, who was 28 years old, could continue his military training. But the move also created the opportunity for the pair to socialize with other members of an aristocratic class that endured despite its formal loss of power following the First World War. Berthold's namesake uncle lived in Berlin, for example.

So did Cäsar von Hofacker, an older cousin of the brothers. This World War I veteran and lawyer had supported the rising Nazi regime from its beginning. In the spring of 1933, after Hitler had become chancellor, Hofacker had publicly endorsed the party and called for the government to establish a dictator-ship and "do away with elections once and for all." At that time he and his wife, Ilse-Lotte, had three children—including Christa, their youngest at just a year old—and they would eventually have two more.

During the 1930s Hofacker served as an attorney in Berlin for a German steel company. His work provided his family with a privileged lifestyle that included a villa staffed with servants. A governess helped care for the children, and the couple hosted elegant

Cäsar von Hofacker pauses during a stroll with his younger daughters, Christa (left) and Liselotte, Berlin, 1942.

dinner parties. Christa watched ladies arrive wearing full-length ball gowns for the evening affairs, accompanied by men dressed in black-tie formal wear. On weekends she sometimes joined her father and older brother and sister on outings into the countryside.

All that came to an end during 1939.

That September, when Christa was seven years old, Hitler started what would become the Second World War by invading Poland. This act of aggression changed family life across Germany. Career soldiers like Berthold's father headed for the front lines, of course, but so did the day laborers who exchanged their tools for rifles. Judges took off their robes to become wartime administrators, and corporate executives were assigned posts as military leaders, including Christa's father, who became a reserve officer. The next year, after Germany overran France, Hofacker was sent to Paris to help manage the occupying government. After that, with one exception years later, the family only saw him during his annual two-week-long military leave. The same held true for Berthold and for countless other children whose fathers had gone to war.

Friedrich-Wilhelm von Hase was born a few years after Christa and Berthold, so his earliest recollections began with the conflict. At first the boy's father, Paul von Hase, had been largely absent from home, directing infantry troops on the front lines in Poland and France. But in 1940, when the youth whom everyone called Friewi was three years old, his father returned to Berlin. Friewi's father had developed heart trouble and needed a job away from combat. Hase assumed command of the capital's defensive forces and moved with his wife and children into a spacious apartment in the stately commandant's headquarters of his post.

The family's experiences there filled Friewi with memories. Servants took care of their personal needs, and the young child

Paul and Margarethe von Hase (seated) with their four children (from left), Maria-Gisela, Friedrich-Wilhelm (Friewi), Ina, and Alexander, summer 1938

watched soldiers salute his father wherever he went. Guards befriended the boy and taught him how to salute too. Staff members entertained Friewi when he visited the commandant's kitchen. Distinguished guests fussed over him when he greeted them in his pressed and proper sailor suit. Sometimes Friewi joined the family on the headquarter's ceremonial balcony where they watched troops parade past on Berlin's grand city-center boulevard, Unter den Linden. "It was very impressive," he recalled years later. "As a child, I saw one aspect of the regime. Nothing else. Only this."

Youngsters throughout Germany were absorbing similar scenes and an accompanying message of stirring nationalism. Word by word, dose by dose, Nazi propaganda reinforced the importance of loyalty to Hitler and his regime, whether in the schools, or through mandatory youth programs, or with state-controlled news media. Friewi was captivated by Nazi news broadcasts about military victories. So was the Stauffenberg boy Berthold, who was three years older.

"Of course I believed in the propaganda and the *Endsieg*"—the idea that Germany would ultimately win the war—"more or less becoming a little Nazi," he later observed.

"Nazism permeated the flesh and blood of the people," noted Professor Klemperer. Key words and expressions "were imposed on them in a million repetitions and taken on board mechanically and unconsciously." Adults who resisted this indoctrination and questioned the regime did so cautiously. They knew that Hitler's Gestapo recruited residents to inform on their neighbors. People worried that agents were listening in on their phone calls. Even as a child, Berthold noted, "one realized, if only vaguely, what could happen if one did not play along." He added that "even the youngest were molded into willing parts of the machinery through a skillful mixture of propaganda and experience, accompanied by a constant feeling of subtle threat."

The pattern repeated itself throughout the country. Lies and fear. Lies and fear.

Not all families believed the lies or supported Hitler, including landowner and farmer Ulrich-Wilhelm Graf von Schwerin von Schwanenfeld. This count had rejected Hitler and Nazism from the beginning. He aligned himself early on with others who disapproved of the man's dishonest speeches, racist beliefs, and brutal tactics. His outrage intensified after he learned of atrocities taking place during the 1939 invasion of Poland. His family held historic claims to considerable property in the region, and he heard firsthand about groups of Polish Christians and Jews being summarily executed at a gravel quarry on his estate. The reports sickened him and spurred his continuing efforts to resist Nazi rule by forming secret alliances with other dissidents.

At the same time, for his own preservation and that of his family, Schwerin feigned loyalty and carried on with his wartime responsibilities as a German military reserve officer.

And that meant his children played their roles as dutiful followers of the regime. When his oldest child, Wilhelm, reached the age of 10, he joined the mandatory Hitler Youth program even though he knew its propaganda contradicted the beliefs of his family. Over time the boy learned to mask his objections to the authoritarian group. "Opposition was not welcome," he observed later. "Contradiction was usually punished with penalties and extra drills."

After invading Poland in the fall of 1939, German troops rolled across western Europe the next spring. Then, in 1941, Hitler ordered an assault to the east against the Soviet Union. In order to monitor the progress of this new campaign, he established a special command center near the eastern front: Wolfsschanze, or the Wolf's Lair. Similar outposts had ties to other military campaigns—Felsennest (Cliff Nest) near the western front and Werwolf (Werewolf) in nearby Ukrainian territory, for example—but the Wolf's Lair quickly became the dictator's favorite military hideaway.

Hitler enjoyed its remote wooded location so much that he ordered repeated improvements to the site. In time the Wolf's Lair complex would expand to fill a square mile with as many as 80 structures. Multiple aboveground pyramid-shaped concrete bunkers rose within the forested landscape to serve as protection during any attack. Surrounding property included a dedicated rail line so that Hitler could travel there by his private train. Related airfields provided easy access for military advisers and for Hitler's own flights. Over time the compound swelled until hundreds of soldiers and support staff lived there and worked to meet his needs.

All that hustle and bustle, all that military might, all that security and protection reinforced Hitler's sense of command. And it made him feel safe. A carpenter named Georg Elser had

German soldiers march through the streets of Warsaw after seizing control of the Polish capital, September 1939.

tried to blow him up at a political gathering in Munich during November 1939. That man was no longer a threat; Hitler had ordered him to be locked away indefinitely at a special prison within Sachsenhausen concentration camp. But one could never be too careful. The Wolf's Lair, located in the middle of wilderness some 300 miles northeast of Berlin, was about as insulated as a hideout could be. So Hitler stayed there with increasing frequency and strayed less and less into public view.

And why should he appear in public? The cult of his personality had become so strong that his mere existence satisfied the general population. Goebbels, his propaganda minister, assured the flow of a relentless stream of intoxicating messages and manipulative reports about Hitler and the regime. And his authoritarian Gestapo police state used spies and crackdowns to stamp out any dissent. The lies, the fear, the grand conquests, the evidence of Germany's might—it all added up to a Nazi machine that hummed along splendidly.

And Hitler, ensconced at its center, seemed invincible.

Members of the Iron Front demonstrate in support of German democracy while displaying a defaced Nazi Party flag, Berlin, May 1, 1932. The three arrows sewn across the swastika symbolized the group's opposition to fascism, communism, and imperialism.

CHAPTER 2

Resisting the Regime

"The German people must and will liberate themselves
from a system that commits terrible crimes under the protection
of terror, and has destroyed the rights, honor,
and freedom of the German people."

Carl Friedrich Goerdeler
Member of the German resistance, May 1943

That was the crux of the problem: Hitler seemed invincible. The people who opposed him faced the same conundrum that challenges anyone trapped in an authoritarian regime: What can you do when one person has that much control? How do you bring down a dictator? Hitler had built much more than a Wolf's Lair of refuge from attack. And he had more than lies and fear on his side. He also had the military. As long as soldiers honored their pledge to protect him, he didn't just seem invincible.

He was invincible.

Moment to moment it could be difficult for some Germans to recognize exactly what was happening around them. After the regime ended, individuals could look back and grasp the fuller picture, but that perspective was harder to achieve during the incremental creep of fascism into their lives. Even many of those who disapproved of aspects of Nazi policy had originally believed that Hitler was himself a rational man. They concluded that the flaws they saw in the government were isolated problems, not symptoms of the dictator's own beliefs and shortcomings. They assumed that Hitler could be reasoned with if he understood the facts. They hoped that his governance would improve and that he would weed out its more unsavory and criminal elements.

It took time for most Germans to come to terms with the nature of the man who had assumed authoritarian control over their country. Such awareness had to dawn individual by individual, and years could pass before someone perceived Hitler's full range of deceit, criminality, and madness. In many cases a fog of propaganda and fear clouded people's minds for the duration of his rule and even beyond.

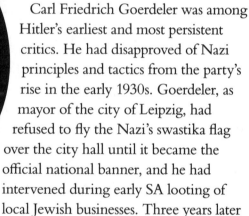

Carl Friedrich Goerdeler was among Hitler's earliest and most persistent critics. He had disapproved of Nazi principles and tactics from the party's rise in the early 1930s. Goerdeler, as mayor of the city of Leipzig, had refused to fly the Nazi's swastika flag over the city hall until it became the official national banner, and he had intervened during early SA looting of local Jewish businesses. Three years later he'd resigned his post as mayor in protest over unsavory practices in the regime. "Hitlerism is poison for the German soul," he wrote soon afterward. Goerdeler spent the rest of his life quietly building connections between others who opposed the dictatorship, but for a long time he still believed that Hitler could be persuaded to make reforms.

Carl Friedrich Goerdeler, undated

Gen. Ludwig Beck also presumed that the dictator would change his mind if he could be presented with logical, fact-based reports. As the army's chief of staff he tried for months during 1938 to warn Hitler that his plans for seizing foreign lands could lead to an unwinnable war. Beck wrote memo after memo on the subject, but Hitler rejected all evidence that contradicted his wishes, and he began screaming during a conference of generals when two of them counseled against going to war. Beck, disheartened, resigned from his post. He retired from the military soon after, unwilling to have his reputation tied to what he felt sure was a doomed campaign filled with senseless death. In the following years he watched his predictions come true. And he collaborated with Goerdeler and others who opposed the regime.

Ludwig Beck, undated

Chinks in the military armor of allegiance to Hitler began to emerge in 1941 after Germany's invasion of the Soviet Union. Many officers objected to the so-called Commissar Order, a Nazi command to kill Communist Party officials who were embedded with Soviet troops. This practice violated well-established international rules of military combat. But German soldiers were only allowed to stop these executions after they were shown to strengthen, not weaken, the fighting morale of Soviet soldiers.

An additional wave of killing accompanied the Third Reich's advance across the eastern front. SS officers followed behind the army and slaughtered thousands of local citizens in the newly captured territory. At times they co-opted German soldiers to help. In many cases local residents were rounded up and shot, then buried in mass graves. Later on they also employed mobile gas chambers that could be driven from site to site. SS officers and their associated police units primarily targeted Jews, including women and children, but they also killed political leaders, clerics, intellectuals, and gypsies. Ultimately, as many as two million innocent people perished in the slaughter.

Propaganda hid the regime's atrocities from the general public, but reports of the combat-zone murders began to spread within the leadership corps of the German military. In subsequent years officers also started to hear about the systematic SS-led genocide of Jewish people at Nazi death camps. Such revelations prompted some officers to turn on Hitler, and these men started to engage in private conversations with trusted comrades about what could be done to stop him.

Propaganda also obscured something else that military commanders were increasingly realizing: Germany was losing the war. From the earliest days Hitler had personally overseen its direction, and he was proving to be a lousy strategist. He did what he wanted to do regardless of the advice or objections of his military advisers. Hitler's invasion of the Soviet Union in 1941 had become a debacle, but he refused to rethink his plans. He ordered troops to persist in that year's campaign despite formidable Soviet defenses and the early arrival of bitter winter weather.

The cumulative results were devastating not only for Russians but for Germans too. Waves of invading soldiers starved or froze to death because of insufficient supplies and inadequate clothing. As the multiyear campaign dragged on, nearly two million German soldiers were captured, killed in combat, or died because of harsh conditions. Military commanders were infuriated by Hitler's mismanagement of this conflict and those on other fronts. Germany's armed forces were being asked to advance or hold territory in too many places. Troops were spread too thin. Commanders were forced to implement doomed orders that led to senseless casualties. Oath of allegiance or not, some officers began to plan for Hitler's demise.

Henning von Tresckow (far right) rides with members of the Ninth Infantry Regiment of Potsdam, Germany, May 30, 1933. Many officers from this unit later joined him in opposing Hitler.

Henning von Tresckow was one of them. While a teenager, he had served in the military during the closing years of the First World War. Later on he had trained to join the officer corps at the same time that Hitler was rising to power. Tresckow's initial hopes for Nazi rule faded quickly. He was repulsed by the nationwide attacks on Jewish people, their property, and synagogues in November 1938, known as Kristallnacht, or the Night of Broken Glass. His disgust grew with Hitler's blundering moves in the Soviet Union, and it intensified after he realized that atrocities were being ordered in these occupied territories.

During 1941 Tresckow began plotting to kill Hitler. By then he had advanced in rank and influence until he'd become a respected colonel in the army's general staff leadership corps. At the same time he had maintained a sphere of influence among an increasing number of officers who were becoming similarly disenchanted with the regime. These men had connections to other disaffected officers in a decentralized but expanding web of shared resolve: Stop the madness.

In addition to being at the hub of discontent among the military's officer corps, Tresckow also served as a link to like-minded people beyond it. Key contacts included Ludwig Beck, the general who had opposed going to war in the first place, and Carl Friedrich Goerdeler, the outspoken former

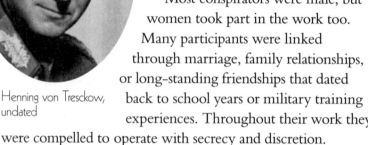

Leipzig mayor. These men had ties to other influential German civilians who shared their opposition to the regime. For the next two years these loosely linked factions struggled to pull together all the elements required for ending Nazi rule.

Most conspirators were male, but women took part in the work too. Many participants were linked through marriage, family relationships, or long-standing friendships that dated back to school years or military training experiences. Throughout their work they

Henning von Tresckow, undated

were compelled to operate with secrecy and discretion. Otherwise they risked being unmasked and harmed.

The complexity of the challenge they faced helps account for the lag between resolve and action. So many questions needed to be considered and answered. Should Hitler be killed, or should he be arrested? Goerdeler was among those who thought it was immoral and hypocritical to employ Nazi-style violence to end the regime. Others felt it was inevitable. If they did decide to kill Hitler, how would they do it? The dictator had become so isolated that there were few opportunities for willing assassins to even reach him. And if they killed him, who else would need to be murdered at the same time? If they only killed Hitler, then his loyal deputies could simply step forward to take his place. If they succeeded in crippling the leadership team, would the military stand by the

34

old government or back the rebellion? Commanders who supported the plot would have to be in place with reliable troops that would enforce the takeover of Nazi operations.

These questions only addressed how to achieve an overthrow, or coup. There were countless others that related to its consequences. For example, would foreign countries respect the rebel's efforts to create a post–Hitler government? Conspirators held multiple secret foreign meetings with international contacts in an attempt to gain favorable terms of surrender. But the Allies never warmed to such entreaties, in part because they questioned the trustworthiness and capabilities of their German contacts. Instead, they preferred to fight for the country's unconditional surrender.

Despite this lack of foreign support, Hitler's opponents continued their work and tried to envision life after the regime. They wanted to avoid repeating the chaos that had followed World War I, and they painstakingly drafted proposals for how to establish a stable democracy. As for who would lead it, Goerdeler topped everyone's list as its first chancellor.

Tresckow did not set aside his determination to kill Hitler while these debates took place. When presented with access to the dictator, he tried to act. In mid–March 1943 he collaborated with others to place a parcel of explosives on the führer's airplane. They managed to load the package by claiming it was a gift of French liqueur for an officer at the plane's destination. But after becoming airborne, the package's triggering mechanism failed to work properly in the high–altitude cold, and the plane landed without it exploding. (Conspirators managed to retrieve the failed device before it was discovered.)

Eight days later Tresckow coordinated a plan to attack Hitler during an inspection of captured military equipment. A colonel assigned to accompany the dictator through the exhibition volunteered to blow himself up while they were together. But that attempt failed too. The suicide bomber was

Hitler, flanked by Heinrich Himmler (second from left) and Hermann Göring, inspects captured Russian weapons, Berlin, March 21, 1943. Col. Rudolf-Christoph Freiherr von Gersdorff (second from right, in the background) was thwarted that day in his attempt to assassinate the dictator.

wired with devices set to explode in 10 minutes' time, but Hitler raced through the exhibition hall so quickly that he departed before the timed devices could detonate. The would-be assassin saved himself by defusing the explosives in a nearby bathroom. Later that year a similar plan was foiled when Allied bombers destroyed some equipment that Hitler was slated to inspect in the company of a different assailant.

Meanwhile, the war continued. Most senior military officers remained loyal to Hitler, and the colonels and other junior officers ready to oppose him could only do so much to unseat the regime. Their day jobs required them to show up for the fight and try to protect soldiers from unwise battle plans. "Our primary role, as officers, was to make sure our men survived and returned home," a conspirator named Philipp Freiherr von Boeselager explained years later.

Other elements of resistance bubbled up in German society, too, as the regime endured. People sheltered Jewish residents from capture and persecution. They shielded conspirators from detection. They disobeyed laws that forbid them to listen to foreign radio broadcasts—an offense that could be punished by imprisonment or even death—and they passed along Allied news reports that contradicted the official propaganda. Resisters with access to military secrets warned the Allies about upcoming wartime operations. Groups of people gathered to secretly discuss their views, plan ways to share them, and organize actions against the regime. Some of these circles were made up of like-minded teenagers. Others formed through university connections or among trusted friends and colleagues.

Anyone who participated in such activities knew they faced severe punishment if caught, and those who were discovered paid dearly. More than 130 German resistance men and women were unmasked in 1942 as part of what the Nazis dubbed the Red Orchestra. Members of this group had passed military secrets to the Allies, including Soviets. They had also protected Jewish residents from persecution and distributed leaflets that corrected the regime's propaganda. More than 60 of them died after being apprehended. Most were tried without due process and sentenced to death by hanging, beheading, or firing squad. Others took their own lives or perished after being sentenced to probationary service on the battlefront.

Among those tied to the Red Orchestra group was an American-born professor named Mildred Fish-Harnack; she had been one of its leaders with her German husband, Arvid Harnack. Her husband was executed three months after being captured. Mildred was initially sentenced to six years of imprisonment, but then Hitler intervened. He wanted greater revenge. Hitler personally revoked the outcome of her trial and ordered a new judicial review. This contrived proceeding led to her beheading in Berlin during February 1943.

Arvid Harnack and Mildred Fish-Harnack, undated

Similarly grim fates befell students in Munich that same month after Nazis uncovered their White Rose group. The university students had produced a series of educational leaflets that they secretly placed around the city and at more distant locations. They hoped their words would spark wider resistance to a regime that they characterized as murderous and "a dictatorship of evil." After key leaders of the effort were caught, they were tried and immediately beheaded. Among those killed were 21-year-old Sophie Scholl and her older brother, Hans. They died within days of Mildred Fish-Harnack.

●┄┄┄┄●┄┄┄┄●┄┄┄┄●┄┄┄┄●

Death was everywhere. As the war entered its fifth year, it became increasingly difficult for propaganda to explain away the growing challenges in everyday lives. Germans didn't need secret leaflets and resistance circles to recognize their changing reality. Food was running short. So were fuel and other supplies. But even in the face of these hardships the population largely kept faith in the Nazi narrative that their nation would triumph in the end, that an *Endsieg,* or final victory, would be the reward for their personal sacrifices. Many believed it was far better to suffer through more combat than to endure another round of harsh consequences such as those that had followed the country's defeat after the First World War.

Germans who lived in cities faced an added terror as the war continued: bombs. Urban attacks had always been a possibility, but they became more frequent over time as a way to undermine local support for the regime. In 1941 the United States had joined the Allied fight against Germany, and the next year British and American bombers started firebombing civilian targets. Ludwig Beck had predicted from the beginning that it would become impossible for Germany to indefinitely muster the necessary personnel and supplies to fight multiple adversaries on multiple fronts. He had known what others were learning: Starting a war was a lot easier than winning one.

By 1943 the soldiers and pilots tasked with protecting Germany's cities simply did not have enough ammunition or defensive aircraft to stop all the Allied bombers. When it became possible for Allied planes to cruise at lower and lower altitudes without meeting sustained resistance, they were able to dump their explosives with greater accuracy and devastating effect, even in the capital of Berlin. That spring, for example, fighters attacked the neighborhood where Christa von Hofacker's family lived. She recalled how "it was carpeted

A banner headline from the *New York Post* about the bombing of Berlin, published March 2, 1943. Royal Air Force (RAF) pilots served Great Britain.

with bombs. Our dearest neighbors all got killed." Her father happened to be in town for meetings at the time of this attack, and his response was swift and decisive. "He moved us within twenty-four hours, and we never went back." The family relocated to a simple home in a town called Krottenmühl nestled far to the south in the Bavarian foothills of the Austrian and Swiss Alps.

Friewi von Hase, the young boy whose family lived in the commandant's headquarters in Berlin where his father worked, learned to follow the steps that accompanied each aerial attack. First the sirens wailed their warning cry of impending bombardments. Then his family scurried to shelter at the deepest levels of the massive structure where they lived. When they emerged after receiving the all-clear signal, they

Cäsar and Ilse-Lotte von Hofacker with their five children (from left), Alfred, Liselotte, Eberhard, Christa, and Anna-Luise, circa 1942–43

The commandant's headquarters, Berlin, December 1937. An Allied air raid set fire to the nearby cathedral dome (far left) in 1943 during the period when Paul von Hase worked and lived at the headquarters with his family.

faced a blackened horizon pierced by the beams of search-lights scanning for more enemy planes.

At the same time that bombs destroyed Christa's neighborhood, they also wreaked havoc near the Hase residence. Afterward Friewi and his family watched from the roof of their building as flames engulfed the domed rotunda of the neighboring cathedral. Such incidents prompted Friewi's parents to send him away. As had been the case with Christa's father, they wanted to protect him from the terror and danger of the attacks. Paul and Margarethe von Hase placed their son in the safekeeping of a close family friend who lived in quieter part of the country.

Berthold von Stauffenberg, the boy whose father had been engaged in officer's training during Hitler's rise to power, had returned to southwestern Germany with his mother and siblings after the war began. His father, Claus von Stauffenberg, had spent the earliest months of the war on the front lines, but the junior officer's exceptional planning and organizational skills led to his transfer to various posts with the military's central command staff. As the war continued, Stauffenberg became increasingly troubled by reports of Nazi war crimes and by Hitler's combat blunders. When he began raising his concerns with fellow officers around 1942, he found some like-minded listeners but little support for action. "The men are wetting their pants or have sawdust in their heads," he observed.

Claus von Stauffenberg (wearing eye patch) recuperates after his injuries in North Africa at his family's estate in Lautlingen, Germany, summer 1943. Three of his four children are with him (Heimeran, far left; Valerie, second from left; and Franz-Ludwig, far right) along with the children of his brother Berthold (Elisabeth and Alfred).

In frustration, and out of fear that his out-
spokenness might lead him to be charged
with treason, the combat veteran asked to
be transferred back to the fighting front.
This request nearly cost him his life. In
early 1943 he found himself in North
Africa helping to manage Germany's
retreat from the advance of Allied
troops. Less than two months later he
was gravely wounded during an air
attack. In addition to sustaining head
trauma and injury to a knee, he lost his
right hand, the last two digits on his other
hand, and his left eye.

Friedrich Olbricht,
undated

Stauffenberg's injuries ended his combat service but not his
military career. He spent months in treatment and recovery,
including a lengthy break for recuperation with his family at
their ancestral home in Lautlingen. But at the end of the summer the 35-year-old was transferred back to Berlin. This move
came with official responsibilities, but it also included secret
duties. Opposition to Hitler had grown among junior officers
during his absence, and the timing seemed right for action.
A sympathetic general named Friedrich Olbricht arranged for
Stauffenberg to become his new chief of staff.

And then the general ordered him to start plotting a coup.

Heinrich Graf von Lehndorff-Steinort swings with daughter Vera, circa 1943–44. This count joined Nazi resistance efforts after witnessing wartime atrocities during Germany's invasion of the Soviet Union.

CHAPTER 3

Valkyrie

"The most terrible thing is to know that
it cannot succeed and that we must nevertheless
do it for our country and our children."

Berthold Schenk Graf von Stauffenberg
Circa July 1944

The plan seemed like it could work. In the weeks following
his transfer back to Berlin, Claus von Stauffenberg collaborated with a talented team to devise a way to kill Hitler and
overthrow his regime. Initially his chief partner was Col.
Henning von Tresckow, the man who had already been
actively trying to assassinate the dictator. The pair of officers
exuded a magnetism and intelligence that made them ideal
leaders of the effort. They undertook their official duties at
the military's central command headquarters in the capital,
a complex known as the Bendler Block, but they pursued
some of their secret work there too.

They and their associates were able to disguise much of
their activity by pretending to update a military operation
known as Valkyrie (pronounced VAL-ka-ree). The original
plan had been named after battle maidens from Norse mythol-
ogy, and it contained standing orders on how soldiers should
respond if Germany ever came under attack. Many of its
defense plans were easy to repurpose, so the team adapted and

revised Valkyrie until it became a blueprint for toppling Hitler's government.

Acting with great secrecy, they and others planned for far more than the movements of rebel troops. The group also evaluated methods for assassinating Hitler and key aides. After considerable study they decided to use explosives with a suicide bomber. The conspirators also drafted goals for the coup and used them to enlist additional participants. They recruited officers with trustworthy troops who would

follow orders to turn on the regime after Hitler's death. They devised ways to seize local radio stations and wrote statements that could be broadcast during the coup to rally the support of German citizens. The group intended to cease fighting with the Allies immediately and hoped to be permitted to enact their plans for a new civilian government.

Tresckow and Stauffenberg had a discreet network of support, both within the military and beyond.

Cäsar von Hofacker, Paris, France, undated

Many conspirators came from Germany's most prominent families. Others were drawn from churches, industry, labor, universities, and banned political groups. They were further aided by civilian activists, family members, close friends, and trustworthy fellow soldiers. Long-standing Nazi critics Beck and Goerdeler became involved. So did Claus's older brother Berthold. So did the von Stauffenbergs' cousin, Cäsar von Hofacker, who was Christa's father. Friewi's father, Paul von Hase, joined the effort too. So did Wilhelm Schwerin

Paul von Hase, undated

von Schwanenfeld's father, the count with land in
Poland who had been opposed to Hitler from
the beginning.

Conspirators knew that it wouldn't be
sufficient to seize control of only Berlin.
To succeed, the coup would need to upend
the Nazi command structure at key locations around Europe. Gestapo officials,
SS officers, and Nazi Party leaders scattered
across the continent would all need to be
detained as part of the uprising. Christa's
father agreed to make arrests from his post
in Paris. Other sympathetic military officers
were recruited in such places as Prague in the
former Czechoslovakia and in the Austrian capital, Vienna.
Meanwhile, Paul von Hase planned to order his soldiers to
disarm Nazi authorities who remained in the German capital
during the planned bombing of Hitler.

Ulrich-Wilhelm Graf
von Schwerin von
Schwanenfeld, 1943

Some conspirators signed on to help during the earliest
stages of the work. Others learned about it just days before
Valkyrie was put into operation. For added security no one
knew everyone who was involved or all the precise plans.
"We knew our roles by heart, but we didn't know exactly
what the others were to do," recalled participant Philipp
Freiherr von Boeselager, an explosives expert. "That was
perfectly normal; to be effective a conspiracy has to remain
compartmentalized."

Planners had hoped to stage the coup during the fall of
1943, but they were unable to find someone who had both
access to Hitler and a willingness to kill him. The dictator
rarely strayed from his fortified command posts, and few
besides his most loyal associates ever got near him. But the

next year, in June 1944, Claus von Stauffenberg gained an unexpected promotion. His boss's boss, a general named Friedrich Fromm, wanted Claus to become his chief of staff. This new job included an important responsibility: attend key military briefings of Adolf Hitler. Fromm understood that a coup was in the works. Although he didn't actively participate in the planning, he may have requested Stauffenberg's transfer as an indirect way to aid the effort. Whatever his motives, the opportunity was irresistible.

But this new chance to reach Hitler presented a dilemma. By this point Tresckow had gained a promotion and been transferred back to the battlefront, so he was no longer available to help implement a coup in Berlin. His absence left Stauffenberg with competing responsibilities. How could he kill Hitler at one of his distant hideaways and at the same time direct an overthrow of the government back in Berlin?

Stauffenberg's importance as commander was immeasurable. He possessed more than an intimate understanding of the complex Valkyrie maneuvers. He also had true, charismatic leadership abilities. Without his pressure and encouragement, plenty of fellow officers might hesitate to step out of the shadows and perform their assigned roles when the coup began. Stauffenberg, to solve this predicament, devised a way to kill Hitler without killing himself or getting caught, then return promptly to Berlin. It was a precarious plan, but there were no better options.

Yet even as circumstances aligned for Valkyrie to begin, some conspirators started to wonder if the attempt was worth the effort and related perils. There were so many ways the mission could fail. And if it did, those with military ties would undoubtedly be charged with violating their oaths of allegiance to Hitler and face the usual sentence of execution by firing squad. Even if it succeeded, it seemed likely that most civilians and soldiers would brand them as traitors.

By July 1944 it was clear that Hitler's days were numbered. Allied forces had retaken key territory on the coast
of France in their famed D-Day landings. Troops and supplies were pouring in at beachheads in Normandy, making
it possible for American and British soldiers to march west
toward Berlin. Meanwhile, Soviet troops were approaching
Germany's capital from points east.

Why not just leave Hitler's fate to the Allies?

Stauffenberg sent a message to Tresckow at the front:
Should they proceed? Was it worth the danger and sacrifice
this late in the war? His friend and ally replied with an
emphatic yes. "The coup must still be attempted," he
asserted. Countless lives would be saved if the war could
be stopped, and it was morally important for Germans
to try to end the regime. "It is no longer a question of the
practical purpose but that, in the eyes of the world and of
history, the German resistance movement risked their
lives for the decisive pitch. Compared to that, nothing else
matters." And so Stauffenberg and others pressed on with
their Valkyrie plans.

Several opportunities for action soon presented themselves.
At a July 11 meeting Colonel von Stauffenberg was armed
with explosives but refrained from using them because key
Nazi leaders weren't present with Hitler. Conspirators had
wanted to improve the odds of the coup's success by killing as
many top figures together as possible. On July 15, the date of
Stauffenberg's next meeting, organizers launched preliminary
Valkyrie maneuvers so that troops would be well positioned
by the time of the attack. But the colonel's encounter with
the dictator was too brief for action. Olbricht managed to
disguise the unusual military activity as a drill—a test
of the original Valkyrie plan—but the misfire meant that
plotters couldn't start early phases of the plan again without
arousing suspicion.

Even with Olbricht's careful dodge, the entire plot seemed increasingly at risk of discovery. A civilian ally tied to it had been arrested earlier in the month; others were in hiding for fear of being caught, tortured, and forced to reveal the plans. When Stauffenberg learned of his next appointment with Hitler, set for July 20 at the Wolf's Lair, he was resolute. This time he would act no matter what. It was imperative to make the attempt, even if only Hitler could be killed.

Word of the impending launch again passed quietly through the ranks of conspirators. Many kept their involvement in the plot so secret that not even their closest family members knew of their roles. They hoped this discretion would allow their relatives to convincingly maintain their ignorance of the operation if Valkyrie failed, thus protecting them from retaliation by the regime.

A career officer named Georg Alexander Hansen masked his ties to the intended assassination by attending the July 20 christening of his five-day-old daughter, Dagmar, far from Berlin. Albrecht von Hagen, another participant, was a central figure in the plotting and had helped hide the explosives ahead of the attack. But this well-placed reserve officer never divulged his work to his wife.

Irene and Georg Hansen with their sons (from left), Karsten, Hans-Georg, and Wolfgang, 1938. Two daughters, Frauke and Dagmar, were born later.

On the eve of the intended assassination, his
eldest child and namesake was camping
on a Hitler Youth outing near the Baltic
Sea. This 11-year-old boy, like everyone
else in the family, was unaware of the
events that were about to unfold.

Albrecht von Hagen,
June 1944

A few days before the planned attack,
Friewi's mother, Margarethe, had extracted
an admission from her husband of his involvement in the plans. She had been out of town
visiting friends, but when she returned to
Berlin her husband seemed lost in thought.
"Finally he told me that there were plans to assassinate
Hitler," she later recalled. Paul von Hase acknowledged that
the attempt could very well collapse, but that he had to help
even if his efforts cost him his life.

On the evening of July 19, in bold defiance of failure,
Hase toasted to the success of the operation by sharing a
bottle of champagne with his wife and two of their four
children, 20-year-old Maria-Gisela and 19-year-old
Alexander. Friewi was still safely away from Berlin, and
their oldest daughter was married and lived elsewhere.

Tresckow's wife, Erika, was well aware of her husband's
work. Claus von Stauffenberg's wife, Nina, also knew of her
husband's efforts but not the precise details of the plan, its
timing, or his duties. She had no idea he had assumed
responsibility for assassinating Hitler, for example. Unaware
that the effort was about to get under way, she had bid her
husband farewell on July 18, bound for a summer stay with
their children at the family estate in Lautlingen.

Stauffenberg had tried to delay their departure, but he
had been unable to keep his family nearby without revealing
the upcoming plans, so he let them go. On the night of
July 19 he telephoned Nina but could not reach her; Allied

Nina Schenk Gräfin von Stauffenberg with her children (from left), Berthold, Heimeran, Valerie, and Franz-Ludwig, April 1941

bombings had disrupted long-distance communication. He spent the evening instead with his brother Berthold. The pair knew that the next day's mission might fail, but they shared Tresckow's belief that they had to at least try. Their love of country drove them onward, pushing them to show that Germans had themselves tried to end Hitler's immoral and deadly regime.

●·············●·············●·············●·············●

On the morning of Thursday, July 20, 1944, Berthold von Stauffenberg accompanied Claus to the airfield where he was scheduled to board a government courier plane. The brothers hoped to meet again that afternoon at the military's Bendler Block headquarters. Stauffenberg made the two-hour flight to the Wolf's Lair accompanied by fellow conspirator and aide Lt. Werner von Haeften. They landed at about ten

o'clock and were driven to the nearby complex. A series of
meetings followed. Shortly before the planned session with
Hitler, Stauffenberg explained that he wanted to change into a
clean shirt. It was a hot day, and it would have seemed reason-
able to want to freshen up ahead of seeing the führer. When
he asked for Haeften to help him, that request made sense too.
An extra person could undoubtedly make the task easier for
the one-handed, three-fingered Stauffenberg.

The pair retreated into a nearby lounge, but they did not
use this privacy to change clothes. Instead, they prepared for
the detonation of two packages of explosives that had been

Adolf Hitler (center) reviews a map with military advisers at the Wolf's Lair,
May 1942.

concealed in Stauffenberg's briefcase. Stauffenberg, as assassin, insisted on tackling key steps himself, but even with Haeften's help the men struggled with the work. They needed to act quickly, both to reach the meeting on time and to deliver the briefcase before it exploded. Furthermore, the greater their delay, the greater their risk of discovery, for how long could they pretend to be changing a shirt?

In fact, at one point a staffer briefly interrupted the pair to urge them to hurry. It was time for Hitler's meeting. He remained at the doorway and could glimpse the two at work but did not realize what they were doing. By then the men had only armed one of the two packages in Stauffenberg's briefcase. Fearing further discovery, they felt compelled to stop. Haeften hid the unused explosive charge in his own briefcase. Then the men left the lounge, and Stauffenberg proceeded toward the conference with Hitler.

During their previous week's session at the Wolf's Lair, all the windows of the meeting site had been blocked with steel shutters. But on the unusually hot day of July 20 these shutters were flung open to admit cooling breezes. Stauffenberg knew that the open windows would reduce the force of the planned explosion, making it all the more unfortunate that he was entering the building with less firepower than intended. Nonetheless, he joined the two dozen people in the room and requested to be positioned close to Hitler with his briefcase placed conveniently nearby under the conference table. Soon after arriving, he excused himself, saying he was required to make a phone call.

But he left his briefcase behind.

Within minutes he had rejoined Haeften, and the pair awaited the upcoming explosion from a safe distance outdoors. When the charge detonated, its force damaged the meeting site so extensively that Hitler's death seemed certain. Stauffenberg even saw a body being removed from the scene that was

Claus von Stauffenberg (far left) stands with Adolf Hitler (center) and other officials at the Wolf's Lair, July 15, 1944. Five days later he returned to try to assassinate the fascist dictator.

draped with Hitler's cloak. He and his accomplice departed the compound immediately and hastened back to a waiting plane. They wanted to become airborne before security measures might prevent their escape. Then they endured the tedium of the flight back to the capital, anxious to confirm that word of their success had reached Berlin and that Valkyrie maneuvers were under way.

It had been the job of Gen. Erich Fellgiebel, a fellow conspirator stationed at the Wolf's Lair, to signal the start of the coup ahead of Stauffenberg's return. But just as he was preparing to phone his contacts in Berlin, he observed a distressing sight: Adolf Hitler. The dictator was still very much alive. He was bleeding, and his pants had been torn to tatters by the explosion, but he had walked away from the destroyed meeting space. Fellgiebel phoned Berlin anyway, but his brief alert created immobilizing confusion. "Something fearful has happened," he reported to fellow conspirator Gen. Fritz Thiele. "The Führer is alive." Then, afraid of betraying the mission by speaking any longer, he hung up the phone.

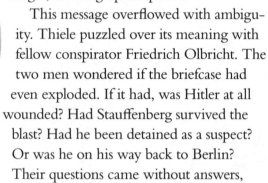

Erich Fellgiebel, undated.

This message overflowed with ambiguity. Thiele puzzled over its meaning with fellow conspirator Friedrich Olbricht. The two men wondered if the briefcase had even exploded. If it had, was Hitler at all wounded? Had Stauffenberg survived the blast? Had he been detained as a suspect? Or was he on his way back to Berlin?

Their questions came without answers, and so they debated what to do next. Maybe the coup should be canceled. Perhaps it was still possible for the plot to remain hidden and for conspirators to evade detection. Absent Stauffenberg's leadership, the men decided to practice an abundance of caution.

Instead of starting a coup, they went to lunch.

● ⋯⋯⋯ ● ⋯⋯⋯ ● ⋯⋯⋯ ● ⋯⋯⋯ ●

After returning to Berlin, Stauffenberg headed to the Bendler Block. He dismissed as Nazi propaganda the reports he heard there of Hitler's survival and urged the coup forward. The multihour delay had been costly, however. Valkyrie orders finally began arriving at far-flung military quarters about the same time as reports from the Wolf's Lair that the dictator was still in charge. Mindful of their loyalty oaths, many conspirators lost their nerve and took no actions to support the uprising. But some stood firm. In Paris, for example, Cäsar von Hofacker and his commanding officer implemented their part of the plan perfectly. By late evening they had successfully rounded up hundreds of Gestapo officials and Nazi SS officers. They had sandbags stacked and ready so that their prisoners could be tried on the spot and shot.

By that time, though, the coup was on the verge of collapse back in Berlin. Conspirators had counted on having the support of Col. Gen. Friedrich Fromm, the man who had placed Stauffenberg in the company of Hitler in the first place. But Fromm refused to help. When he heard counter reports that Hitler remained alive, he turned on the conspirators and

Commandant Paul von Hase (left) and German troops welcome a visiting dignitary to Berlin, July 20, 1941. Exactly three years later he used military forces under his command to support the Valkyrie coup attempt.

The Bendler Block entrance, Berlin, circa 1940

accused them of treason. The rebels responded by arresting him and locking him in a nearby office. They tried to move forward, but their orders didn't command the same respect as Fromm's would have had.

This confusion further undercut the effectiveness of the plan and left key missions unfulfilled. Conspirators failed to make radio broadcasts, for example, and thus lost the opportunity to rally support within the general public. By late evening Nazi loyalists had reached the rebels in the Bendler Block. During a brief exchange of gunfire, Stauffenberg was wounded in his left shoulder. Fromm was soon set free, and the double-crossing general promptly ordered the immediate execution of four key rebels, including Stauffenberg. He agreed to let Ludwig Beck, the retired general who had been working alongside the group, attempt suicide rather than face a firing squad. Fromm's orders not only ended the coup; they also conveniently silenced key people who otherwise could have betrayed his prior knowledge of the plans.

Guards escorted the four prisoners down two double flights of stairs to an interior courtyard. Then they were shot one at a time by a 10-man team of soldiers. In addition to Stauffenberg, others executed that night were his aide Haeften, his previous commander Friedrich Olbricht, and Olbricht's new chief of staff, Albrecht Ritter Mertz von Quirnheim. In a sign of the trouble that lay ahead for anyone found too close to the conspiracy, within hours authorities had detained the man who had ordered their deaths: Fromm was suspected of being in on the uprising too.

The dead conspirators were buried overnight in a mass grave, but within hours workers were dispatched to exhume their bodies. Burial was deemed too honorable an end for those who had defied the rule of Hitler. They were traitors, and traitors earned no memorial. Instead, the corpses of the five men were sent to a crematorium where they were reduced to a comingled silt of dusky powder and chips of bone, then tossed over an open field.

All evidence of their defiance was to be erased without a trace.

The trial of Berthold Schenk Graf von Stauffenberg in the People's Court, Berlin, August 10, 1944. He was pronounced guilty and executed later that day—three weeks after the failed coup and the death of his brother Claus.

CHAPTER 4

Hitler's Revenge

"I speak to you ... so that you may also hear the particulars about a crime that is without peer in German history. An extremely small clique of ambitious, conscienceless, and criminal and stupid officers forged a plot to eliminate me."

Adolf Hitler
Radio broadcast, July 21, 1944

Hitler was furious. Someone had tried to kill him. Again. At his highly fortified Wolf's Lair, of all places. And he had been wounded.

Never mind that he had walked away from the bombing site. His right elbow had been bruised severely when the conference table slammed into his arm. Portions of the heavy oak table had shielded him from the blast, but countless splinters from the rest of it had been propelled like spears into meeting participants, including Hitler. The explosion had singed the back of the dictator's scalp and burned his legs. Like most of the other survivors, his eardrums had been ruptured from the force of the bomb.

But Hitler was also excited that he had survived another attempt on his life. Four other men in the room would not; they died either instantly from their wounds or soon after. Many had received injuries worse than his. Rather than seeing himself as weakened, the dictator regarded the failed attack as the latest proof of his invincibility. "I have been saved," he told a pair of office workers that afternoon. "Destiny has chosen me, providence has preserved me. It is a sign that I must see my mission through to the end." In the dark mind of Adolf Hitler, part of that mission included an obsessive, paranoid determination to exact revenge on his attacker. But revenge on whom?

A man displays the tattered remains of Adolf Hitler's pants after the explosion at the Wolf's Lair, late July 1944.

Before that question could be answered, loyal officers stationed at the Wolf's Lair learned of a more immediate problem: A coup was under way. Confusion swirled throughout the Third Reich for the remainder of the day while dueling orders and counterorders competed for attention. And then the rebellion collapsed. The German public heard about the attempted coup shortly after its failure. Many listened to the late-night radio broadcast Hitler made from the Wolf's Lair to prove he had survived. "I myself am wholly unhurt," he proclaimed falsely. He stated that plotters of the overthrow "are now being mercilessly exterminated."

Propaganda-driven reports repeated the news the next day in local papers and on radio stations for anyone who had missed Hitler's speech. Nina von Stauffenberg learned of her husband's role and fate from an early morning news broadcast.

So did her oldest children. Berthold could not understand why his father would have wanted to kill Hitler. As a child steeped in Nazi propaganda, the idea was inconceivable. He later recalled how "the führer was at least as high as the Emperor had been, and there was sort of adulation. That somebody tried to kill him was outside our imagination." That his father could have been behind the attack was even more unfathomable.

Berthold was not alone in his astonishment. Soon after the explosion an observant young officer at the Wolf's Lair had suggested that circumstantial evidence linked Claus von Stauffenberg to the fatal explosives. Why else had he left the grounds in such haste? On hearing this theory, a senior officer had reprimanded the man for, as historian Peter Hoffmann put it, "voicing so monstrous a suspicion against such a distinguished officer." But the young man's hunch

Hitler broadcasts news of his survival during a 1 a.m. radio address from the Wolf's Lair, July 21, 1944.

SS guards and Nazi leaders, including Hermann Göring (fourth from left), inspect the bombing site at the Wolf's Lair, circa July 21, 1944.

would be confirmed, both by events in Berlin and by detective work back at the Wolf's Lair. When questioned, the driver who had taken Stauffenberg to his departing flight recalled that his aide had tossed a package out of the car during their brief trip. A subsequent search of the roadside woods revealed a discarded bundle of explosive material—the one the pair had failed to arm.

It also became clear that only a series of coincidences had saved Hitler's life. If the conference had taken place in a concrete bunker, if the assassins had managed to trigger both packages of explosives, even if they'd merely left the unwired parcel in the briefcase where it would have been ignited by the force of the initial explosion, Hitler would almost certainly have been killed. There was another detail too. After Stauffenberg had left the meeting room, someone reportedly had moved his briefcase to get it out of the way. The four men who died had ended up being closest to it.

Those few feet seemed to have saved the dictator's life.

In the final hours of the failing coup, conspirators had begun burning incriminating documents. But they hadn't had time to destroy everything, and in the coming days and weeks government investigators began piecing together eye-popping shreds of evidence. Flow charts outlining the decentralized conspiracy. Statements of the principles behind the coup. Names of proposed leaders for the new government. And much more. It soon became clear that the coup had involved far more people than the "small clique" that Hitler had initially described. Nazi officials were astounded as they started to tug at the tangled knot of betrayals. It began to seem that no one was above suspicion. The paper trail led straight to the doors of countless military officers, government servants, and

Nazi SS troops and German soldiers occupy the Bendler Block courtyard, Berlin, July 21, 1944. Just hours earlier Claus von Stauffenberg and three others had been executed there.

civilians. Such revelations added to Hitler's paranoia and fury, not to mention his thirst for revenge.

Some individuals were swept up by Gestapo agents within hours of Valkyrie's collapse. Paul von Hase had been conversing at home with his wife, son Alexander, and daughter Maria-Gisela at about eleven o'clock that night when he was called away for a meeting with Nazi officials. None of the family members ever saw him again. "Without saying goodbye, it was farewell forever," Maria-Gisela later wrote.

After the coup collapsed, Cäsar von Hofacker's commanding officer (and fellow conspirator) had given him the option of fleeing Paris to escape capture, but Cäsar stood by his actions and accepted arrest. Authorities promptly detained Claus von Stauffenberg's brother Berthold, who had been with him at the Bendler Block. Within days they detained the father of 11-year-old Albrecht von Hagen. And the father of teenager Wilhelm Graf von Schwerin von Schwanenfeld. And the father of the newly christened Dagmar Hansen. And more.

Maj. Gen. Henning von Tresckow learned almost immediately that Valkyrie had failed. He wrote a final letter to his wife; then he approached the nearby front lines and killed himself. In an effort to hide his link to the conspiracy and thus protect others, he disguised his death to make it look like he had been hit during an enemy ambush.

Some conspirators avoided arrest by hiding, or surrendering to Allied forces, or trying to appear innocent by staying on the job. Gen. Fritz Thiele, the man who had taken the confusing call from the Wolf's Lair, tried the latter approach, but he was soon unmasked and detained. The intended chancellor, Carl Friedrich Goerdeler, had gone underground before Valkyrie, but by mid-August Nazi authorities had discovered him hiding in Poland and arrested him too. Within weeks some 700 people were swept up and charged.

As investigators sorted through the evidence, they discovered that even Gen. Erwin Rommel, Germany's revered combat tank commander, was in on the conspiracy. He had been seriously wounded during an air strike three days before the coup attempt and thus had been unable to take part in the uprising, but his ties to the effort became unmistakable. Hitler understood that confidence in his regime would be shaken if the public learned that this national hero had turned against him. He ordered Rommel be given a choice: take poison or be disgraced as a traitor and killed. Rommel chose to take the poison. His forced suicide was kept a secret, and his death was attributed to his wounds. The general's decision left his reputation intact, secured his family's safety, and allowed Hitler to exploit the death as propaganda for a celebrated warrior.

Rommel, like other officers in the German military, had probably expected to face trial by a military court martial, if caught, and death by firing squad. But to a furious Hitler bent on revenge, that outcome wasn't sufficient. He wanted the accused men expelled from the armed services so that they could be held to account within his personal corrupt judicial arena: the People's Court. Early in his dictatorship Hitler had established this tribunal as a forum for punishing his political enemies. It operated as a theater of propaganda, not as a proper system with an impartial review of evidence and the option of judicial appeals. By sending the accused to the People's Court, Hitler would ensure everyone viewed the men just as he did.

As traitors.

The paranoid Hitler ordered that the earliest trials and executions be filmed so that he could confirm that proceedings were carried out according to his wishes. He was adamant about the importance of silencing the accused. "They must have no time for speeches!" he insisted, no chance to defend themselves. A fiery bully named Roland Freisler headed the court with a style that met the führer's demands perfectly. He was known for screaming at defendants when they tried to plead their cases and belittling them with withering insults.

The Valkyrie trials began on August 8 and continued for months. The accused rarely managed to be heard in court. Convictions were all but certain, with death the almost inevitable punishment. Sentences were often carried out within hours, or at least within days. Few escaped with their lives. Paul von Hase and seven other men were the first to be tried. His oldest child, Ina, had attempted repeatedly to visit her father, but she was always turned away. On the day of his so-called trial, she wrote an anguished letter to her mother-in-law. "In a few hours, Papi will no longer be with us," she predicted.

Some condemned men were allowed to send parting messages to loved ones. "My most beloved in the world!" Heinrich Graf von Lehndorff-Steinort wrote his wife as he prepared to die. In the multiple pages that followed, the count explained his reasons for supporting the coup, his sorrow at all its consequences, and his regret at being torn away from his family—the youngest of their four daughters had been born after his arrest. "I am unhappy because my heart wants to tell you so much more, but there is no more paper and no more time." He added one final sentence: "It's all just love and love again."

Then he was killed.

As his daughter had feared, Paul von Hase was executed the same day he appeared before the People's Court. So were the others accused alongside him, including Albrecht von Hagen's father. They were the first to perish in a purge that ultimately

Roland Freisler (center) presides over the People's Court during a trial of Valkyrie conspirators, Berlin, undated.

claimed the lives of more than 150 people. Many German historians classify these deaths as murders. Most of the victims were cruelly hanged using wire nooses in the execution chamber of Plötzensee Prison. Their bodies were then sent to the nearby Berlin Institute of Anatomy and later destroyed. No remains were saved for burial or family remembrance.

Some convicted men were held long after they had been condemned to die. Christa's father was imprisoned for months. So were Carl Friedrich Goerdeler and other key conspirators. These extended detentions allowed for repeated interrogations, torture, and cruel treatment, including the terror of not knowing when a death sentence would be carried out. Interrogators tried to trick prisoners into incriminating others by producing faked confessions from fellow inmates. They warned them that their family members might be harmed if they withheld information. Few cracked under such treatments.

Albrecht von Hagen stands before the People's Court during the opening trial of Valkyrie conspirators, Berlin, August 8, 1944. He and seven others were pronounced guilty and executed later that day.

● ············ ● ············ ● ············ ● ············ ●

Hitler had no intention of limiting his revenge to the web of conspirators. From the beginning of his regime he and his deputies had projected guilt by association onto the family members of anyone accused of disloyalty. The practice was described by the German word *Sippenhaft,* which literally means "clan arrest" but is usually translated as "family punishment." Hitler wanted the Sippenhaft policy applied as broadly as possible within the families of the conspirators so that it included the "spouse, children, siblings, parents, and other relatives." As far as he was concerned, they were traitors too.

Nazi authorities wasted no time implementing Hitler's wishes. Even as they apprehended and punished the individuals who had plotted against him, they also began to round up these people's relations. On July 23 young Berthold awoke to learn that his mother and his great-uncle Nux had been arrested during the night by the Gestapo and taken away to some unnamed destination. The next night agents returned to seize the boy's Stauffenberg grandmother and her older sister, his great-aunt Üllas. They also arrested his aunt Mika, the wife of his uncle Berthold, who had been visiting the family property with the couple's children.

With all the adult relatives gone, Berthold, his three younger siblings, and their two cousins found themselves left in the care of their nanny and other servants at the family estate in Lautlingen. Authorities arrested more relatives at other locations. They traveled to Greece to seize the third brother in Claus's family, Berthold's twin, Alexander, who had known nothing about the planned coup. And they arrested this man's wife, Melitta. Soon they held more than two dozen members of the extended family.

SS leader Heinrich Himmler took personal charge of managing the Valkyrie-related Sippenhaft. On August 3, two weeks after the failed coup, he outlined the plan for family punishment during a speech to the Nazi regime's regional administrators. To understand the reason for retaliation, "You only need to read the Germanic sagas," he explained. "When the family was outlawed and banned, they said, 'This man has committed betrayal, his blood is bad, it contains traitor's blood, it will be wiped out.' And with blood revenge it was wiped out down to the last member of the whole clan. The Graf Stauffenberg family will be obliterated down to the last member," he proclaimed to welcoming applause. He later added: "We will allow all those in Germany named Stauffenberg, all those indeed who unfortunately bear names that are involved in this case of betrayal, to apply to change their names, because we cannot expect them to continue bearing the name of a cad and a traitor."

When Joseph Goebbels addressed the group, he used his skills as propaganda minister to emphasize how the plan would be put into effect. The crackdown would be under-taken gradually, he explained, so as not to distress the general public. If too many arrests and deaths happened at once, it could fuel a wave of public outrage and protest. It was essential to avoid "creating extraordinary domestic unrest," he explained. Goebbels also appreciated the propaganda value of an incremental but persistent campaign of arrests. People would begin to worry that they themselves might somehow be at risk. And they would realize that if the regime was willing to jail members of its most elite families, no one was safe. Few would dare to object to the retaliation.

Most members of the German public swallowed these carefully packaged lies. Then they condemned Stauffenberg, his associates, and their families as traitors.

When 11-year-old Albrecht von Hagen returned from his Hitler Youth camping excursion soon after the failed coup, his family still had no idea that his father had been tied to the failed uprising. Accordingly, they rallied behind Hitler. The boy watched his grandfather lead a parade of military veterans in a local show of support. But even before Albrecht's family realized what his father had done, the Gestapo arrived to arrest them. In late July agents took away his grandfather, grandmother, and mother, "without any hint about the what, why, and where," Hagen later recalled. "My sister and I didn't understand it all, of course." The care of the boy and his younger sibling fell by default to their only remaining adult relative, Aunt Anna, "a sickly old lady who just happened to be at the manor house at the time."

When implementing Sippenhaft, the Gestapo agents began by arresting teenagers and adults; mothers, like Albrecht's, were forced to leave their younger children behind. On July 28 agents separated Irene Hansen from her two-week-old infant daughter, Dagmar, the girl who had been christened on the day of the coup, and her four older children. On July 30 they arrested Ilse-Lotte von Hofacker in Krottenmühl along with her two oldest children, ages 16 and 14. When the trio were led away, a Nazi government nurse took charge of Ilse-Lotte's remaining children, 12-year-old Christa and her two younger siblings.

And so it went, family by family, until as many as 200 relatives had been detained. Many of them were imprisoned in Berlin because that was where they had been arrested. Others were scattered around Germany in local jails or regional prisons. A few were sent straight to concentration camps where they were held in quarters isolated from forced-labor prisoners. The 71-year-old parade-leading grandfather of Albrecht von Hagen was dispatched directly to Sachsenhausen concentration camp near Berlin, for example.

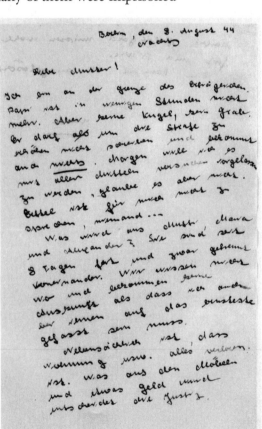

Letter written by Baronin Ina von Medem, eldest daughter of Paul von Hase, to her mother-in-law about her father's impending trial and expected execution, August 8, 1944. "What will happen to Mother, Maria, and Alexander?" she wrote. Fearing the worst, she concluded, "A family has been wiped out."

Just as Hitler had done during earlier crackdowns—such as the 1934 Night of the Long Knives—he used the Valkyrie uprising as a fresh excuse to persecute unrelated enemies. Nazi authorities arrested thousands of people who held no ties to

Berlin-Moabit Prison, November 1938. After Valkyrie, Paul von Hase's wife, eldest son, and youngest daughter were among the family members of conspirators who were detained at the site.

the failed coup. They scooped up family members whose husbands had turned against the German state after being captured by the Soviets. They launched Operation Thunderstorm to seize politicians with ties to the country's disbanded democracy. Authorities cast such a wide net of oppression that they effectively snuffed the life out of any remaining elements of the German resistance.

●·········●·········●·········●·········●

Margarethe von Hase's turn for arrest arrived on August 1. When Gestapo agents escorted her away from the family apartment in the commandant's headquarters, they dissuaded her from bringing a coat. She wouldn't need it, they said, because they would bring her home later that evening. But they did not. Instead, unbeknownst to her, they returned to seize Maria-Gisela and Alexander.

Margarethe found herself confined to death row in the women's section of Berlin-Moabit Prison. "Every night women from the other cells were taken to their executions," she later wrote, unable to forget their screams. When a pastor visited her, "he told me that I, too, would soon be standing before God and gave me a Bible verse for this last journey." And yet as days and weeks passed, no one came to escort her to her death. She measured the passage of time in part by her increasing discomfort while clothed in the summer dress she'd been wearing when arrested. Without a coat she became colder and colder as the season changed into fall.

Meanwhile, her daughter Maria-Gisela was confined to a solitary cell next to the wife of Friedrich Olbricht, one of the four men who had been executed on the night of the failed coup. It took time for the 20-year-old to realize that she could be trapped indefinitely. Some might say, Maria-Gisela later observed, "'The first days are the worst,' but I don't think that's true." To cope with the tedium, she read the scraps of newspaper that were supplied to each prisoner for use as toilet paper. It was by this means that she confirmed news previously whispered to her by another inmate: "Don't cry girl, your father's dead." Mixed within the paper tatters, she found proof in black and white. She later speculated that someone "must have cut out this specific article and passed it on to me."

At the same time, her younger brother Alexander was being held in a nearby men's prison section. His solitary cell measured barely more than a hundred feet square and was lit every hour of the day, even when he tried to sleep. In an effort to occupy his mind, he recited literary passages from memory and tried to multiply three-digit numbers in his head. When guards discovered he had secretly received two books, they beat him up. Then they threatened to shoot him if he reported their abuse. Gestapo agents questioned him about the coup more than once, and they interrogated his mother and sister, too, but all three of them denied knowing about it in advance. None revealed the champagne they had shared to mark the eve of the attack.

On the last day of September, after more than eight weeks in unexplained captivity, Margarethe and her daughter were reunited and discharged from prison. Their releases coincided with those of a number of other relatives of recently executed conspirators. Alexander was dismissed about two weeks later. Instead of being able to rejoin his mother and sister, though, the 19-year-old was required to immediately depart for military service.

The last photo ever taken of the Hayessen family (from left), Hans-Hayo, Egbert, Volker, and Margarete, spring 1944

"When my mother and I came out, we had nothing," Maria-Gisela recounted. Her parents' apartment at the commandant's headquarters had been taken over by the authorities soon after their arrests. Heinrich Himmler and his wife had even slept there for a time, having lost their own residence during an Allied bombing raid. The von Hases' possessions had been pilfered, scattered, or lost. "We had no money,

Certificate of release for Margarete Hayessen from Ravensbrück concentration camp, October 6, 1944. Her detention lasted 68 days.

we had no place to go, we had nothing. We stood on the street and said, 'What now?'" Other families caught up in Sippenhaft were asking the same thing.

What now?

Some relatives were released to discover that their extended families, as was the case with the von Hases, would have nothing more to do with them. Homeless and without supportive relatives, Margarethe and Maria-Gisela sought shelter from a series of family friends. Some detainees, like Alexander von Hase, didn't learn until their release of the fates of the husbands and fathers who had been seized in the wake of the failed coup. Many had lost track of their other arrested relatives and struggled to locate them. Everyone faced the shame of having been branded as traitors. Most frightening of all, when mothers returned to their homes they discovered something dreadful had happened while they were being detained.

Nazi agents had taken away their younger children.

Stauffenberg
Kinder
mit Ea
11·8·1944

From top left: Berthold, Alfred, Heimeran, Franz-Ludwig, Valerie, and Elisabeth Stauffenberg sit with Ester Graf, their nanny, Lautlingen, August 11, 1944. Six days later Gestapo agents apprehended the children for Sippenhaft detention.

CHAPTER 5

The Ghost Children

"[On August 24] that dreadful Gestapo man had appeared at
the door. It was he who had taken the others away.
'I've come on orders from Berlin to fetch the three children.
I'm to take them to a place near Munich today.' His words
had sounded ice-cold, and he made them come true."

Christa von Hofacker, age 12
Diary entry, August 1944

Friewi von Hase was still living with family friends far from
Berlin when Valkyrie occurred. His host, the woman whom
he affectionately called Aunt Ilse, reacted to the news by
taking him on a trip. Years later he realized that she had
probably been trying to protect him from capture, and at first
the ruse had worked. But late one evening, some days after
their return, two Gestapo agents arrived to claim Friewi.
They insisted that the seven-year-old be roused from his sleep
and prepared for immediate departure. The youth watched
Ilse fight back tears as she gathered together some possessions
for him to take on his journey. Then the two men left with
the boy and boarded a train, offering no explanation of where
they were going or what would follow.

During the period when Friewi had been traveling with
Ilse, the world had gone topsy-turvy for young Berthold von
Stauffenberg. His father was dead. His mother was missing.

And two Gestapo agents had begun living in the family home with the remaining young children and the house staff.

By then "there were hate-filled news reports about the conspiracy on the radio and in the newspapers every day," he later recalled. All were reminders that he and his family had fallen from grace, that his fellow Germans viewed them as traitors.

Friedrich-Wilhelm (Friewi) von Hase during a visit to the zoo, Berlin, circa 1943

And then, several weeks after his mother's arrest, orders arrived for the six children to leave home too. "The housekeeper took us to the village priest who gave us his blessing" before their departure, Berthold recalled. "He also told us that we were probably facing hard times, but we should never forget what my father had acted for." The priest's private endorsement of his father's actions amounted to treason. "It was only much later that I realized how courageous these words were," Berthold observed.

During the same period, Christa von Hofacker's home had been invaded by outsiders too. Gestapo agents had taken away her mother and two older siblings. Nurses from the Nazi public welfare system, known as the NSV, had moved in to monitor the care by visiting relatives and friends of the remaining three children—12-year-old Christa and her younger brother and sister. Three weeks later the Gestapo returned to claim these siblings too. Within hours the trio had embarked on what became a three-day, 500-mile journey. Their travels included multiple train transfers, makeshift sleeping, and an encounter with an Allied bombing raid. Throughout there was no explanation of when the journey would end or what might happen next, so mile by mile and day by day the children's anxieties multiplied.

Henning and Erika von Tresckow with their four children (from left), Rüdiger, Adelheid (Heidi), Uta, and Mark, 1941

After authorities uncovered Henning von Tresckow's involvement in the Valkyrie plans, his family was swept up by Sippenhaft too. No detail was too small for the regime's attention. Workers exhumed the soldier's corpse, which previously had been buried on family property with military honors. Then, per the standards Hitler had set for the men who had betrayed him, the body was destroyed. His eldest children, a pair of sons in their mid-teens, were already serving with frontline troops and were left to the hands of fate. (Only one survived the war.) His two younger children were arrested and held for a while in prison with their mother. Then authorities removed Uta, age 13, and her four-year-old sister, Heidi, and launched them on the same cross–country journey that was being made by other youngsters.

The Nazi flag flies over houses at the Borntal numbered (from left) 3, 2, and 1, circa late 1930s. The property included four additional wooden houses and a separate building for medical care.

Throughout August 1944, Gestapo agents scooped children up in ones and twos and even in sibling clusters as large as five, offering no reliable explanation of where they were going or what outcome awaited them. An agent appeared unexpectedly at the Hagen home and told Albrecht and his younger sister he would take them to see their mother. (He did not.) Officials pulled one girl out of a friend's birthday party. They yanked another from the hospital where she was recuperating. Dozens of children were captured, some too young to talk, or even to walk. Most of them did not grasp that they were taken because of the failed coup. Some children actually belonged to families with no ties to the uprising at all. Their parents had merely gotten crosswise with the Nazi regime.

●··········●··········●··········●··········●

Almost all the children were escorted to one spot, a tourist town in central Germany called Bad Sachsa (roughly pronounced Bod SOCKS-sah). *Bad* is the German word for "spa," and the site was famous for its restorative spring waters. But Nazi officials hadn't chosen this destination because of its famous baths; they valued it for entirely different reasons. First, the small secluded town was a perfect place for Nazi authorities to hide the children while they determined their ultimate fates. Second, the community fell inside a federally controlled security zone that made it that much harder for outsiders to reach. Finally, and perhaps most important, the Borntal was there.

The Borntal was a youth retreat that had been founded in 1936 as a rural haven for children from the industrial north. Its name came from ancient words that translate as "spring valley." The property consisted of a cluster of newly built wooden houses and other structures nestled in a forested dell just beyond the northeastern edge of town. Nazi authorities had

Aerial view of the Borntal property with buildings labeled, undated. ISO stands for the isolation ward, or infirmary building.

taken control of the facility almost immediately after it opened, folding it into the regime's NSV social welfare system. By 1944 it had become a residential training center for young nurses and was home to as many as 200 children and teens.

After the failed coup, Nazi officials ordered manager Elli Köhler to vacate the space and prepare for new residents—the offspring of traitorous Germans. The staff she retained was sworn to secrecy about their new assignment, and by mid-August they were ready to receive the detained children. This period of reconfiguring helps account for the delayed arrest and transport of the youngsters to Bad Sachsa.

During their traumatic travels, Christa von Hofacker had tried to reassure her younger siblings, but as soon as the trio reached the Borntal she lost that right. "Three caretakers appeared, and each one took one of us away," she recorded in her diary. "We were separated." So were other sets of siblings. Family ties no longer mattered. Instead, children were grouped by age and gender within the various houses on the property.

The last photo ever taken of Cäsar von Hofacker with his children (from left), Liselotte, Christa, Eberhard, Alfred, and Anna-Luise, April 1944

When Christa happened upon her nine-year-old brother, Alfred, at the office two days later, "he was in terrible despair," she observed. "I tried to help him, but I had nothing at all cheerful to tell him, for the future that lay before us was gray and dark. We were soon torn apart again by Miss Köhler, the home manageress, and Alfred took his leave from me, bravely swallowing his tears."

Liselotte, Christa's younger sister, became catatonic from the shock of this final deprivation. She'd been separated from her father, then her mother, her eldest siblings, and finally Christa and Alfred. According to Christa, "She didn't let anybody touch her. She didn't eat. She didn't go to the bathroom. Nothing. She was just staring straight ahead." Despite their isolation, Christa tried to reassure her sister whenever possible, even just waving to her when she was escorted past her sister's residence. But the trauma took hold and never fully let go.

Mental health professionals now recognize that children faced with such circumstances are often too young to understand the causes behind their suffering. They may be unable to grasp that their loved ones were forced to leave them behind; instead, they feel abandoned and unwanted. They may even conclude that their change of circumstance is some sort of personal punishment.

The behavior of Borntal employees compounded the confusion of arriving children. Staff members acted as if there was nothing out of the ordinary about the youngsters' stay. They provided the illusion of reliable care—including three wholesome meals a day—while implementing a system of strategic harassment. Staffers ignored the peculiarity of the fact that the boys and girls were being held against their will. And that their luggage had been ransacked to remove family photographs and other personal items. And that the children's last names had been changed.

Severing family ties became a signature element of Sippenhaft at the Borntal. All the children were prohibited from
using their families' last names and were assigned replacement
surnames. Uta von Tresckow was told to call herself Uta
Wartenberg. Christa was informed that she was not a
Hofacker. She and her siblings were required to use the last
name Franke. Albrecht von Hagen was renamed Albrecht
Schultz. Berthold and his siblings
became Meisters instead of
Stauffenbergs, and their cousins
were called the Schneiders. And
so it went from family to family
until the detained children had
lost not just their personal control, parents, homes, belongings,
and siblings.

Their very identities were at risk.

Albrecht von Hagen and his
sister, Helmtrud, circa 1941

"These first few days were terrible, desolate, and grueling,"
Christa later recorded in her diary. "One question after
another arose in me: 'Where is Father—does he know about
us—is he still alive? Are the others still in Munich, have they
survived the [recent air raid] attacks? And—what is to become
of us?!? Oh, God, why this suffering?'"

As a 12-year-old girl from a privileged background in Nazi
Germany, Christa had the innocence of someone who had
grown up trusting the adults and systems that surrounded her.
Government propaganda ensured that she was unaware of the
regime's atrocities, and she had been trained to believe that
Germany would win the war. In a matter of weeks, her world
had imploded.

She was old enough to understand that her father had
turned against Hitler and that this decision could cost him his

life. But she could not explain what had happened since. Even though she was one of the older children held at the Borntal, she couldn't fathom why this particular collection of girls and boys had been brought together. Nor, given the terror of uncertainty that shadowed them, could she or the others be sure of what might happen next. The group of captives quickly realized they would receive no help from the stern Nazi-pin-wearing Miss Köhler. Nor did they learn anything from the young women who staffed the residences.

The detained children were not enrolled in local schools, nor did they receive any lessons. They never visited the nearby community, not even to attend church. Instead, every effort was made to keep them hidden and to prevent contact with local residents. They were not permitted to go outside without being accompanied by a caregiver, and when out of doors they were forbidden from speaking. Over time the youngsters invented their own unique sign language so they could communicate with one another in silence.

A few children arrived at the Borntal after August, including Wilhelm von Schwerin von Schwanenfeld, the teen who had become adept at going through the motions of Hitler Youth activity. He and his younger brother Christoph had initially been taken with their mother to the workhouse of a rural prison. But in mid-September they were told it was time to return to school. Instead of being escorted back to classes, though, Gestapo agents had taken the brothers to Bad Sachsa. At age 15 Wilhelm became the oldest of a group that now had grown to number 44 children from 18 families.

"Life in the home was like being locked up, but it was bearable because

Wilhelm Graf Schwerin von Schwanenfeld (left) and his brother Christoph, summer 1941 we received hardly any rules or instruction on how to behave," observed Wilhelm. The calm environment and repetitive patterns of the children's everyday existence may have helped the time pass, but they did nothing to address the unanswerable questions: *Why am I here? How long will I stay? What will happen next? What is happening to my siblings? Are my parents all right? Will I ever see them again?*

Am I safe?

Such worries pulsed through their minds as reliably as a heartbeat. They echoed in their heads as repetitively as the bells that rang in the church towers of the nearby town. The uncertainty swirled and festered in endless mental loops, depriving the children of their sense of security. "There are some people who can support this better than others," Friewi later observed. All alone after having been separated from his parents, older siblings, and even Aunt Ilse, he found that "knowing nothing about their fate was a heavy burden." Christa was able to find some solace by confiding in her diary. "Thinking of Father helped me a great deal," she wrote, "for he too would be suffering and would always look the future bravely in the eye."

One way the children coped with their confinement was to reclaim their names. "Listen, Christa, let's stop this," Uta said privately to her roommate some days after their arrival. "I think we've both been pussyfooting around. My mother is in prison, and yours probably is too!" Christa described in her diary how she and Uta "simultaneously broke the bolts that had kept our hearts locked! We were able to tell each other everything, each unburdening her heart to the other and feeling suddenly light."

Other children began to talk and to share their names too. One of the boys told Friewi that he could call him Nicolai Müller if he wanted, "but that his real name was Nicolai

Bad Sachsa police registration record for Stauffenberg children held at the Borntal, issued May 8, 1945. The document shows both the false last names assigned to the six children (shown in column one) and their real surnames (final column).

Freytag von Loringhoven—and besides, this very name was also written out in marking ink on the inside of his Lederhosen." Friewi recalled: "I remember vividly that Nici proceeded to show me this overlooked proof of his real identity with a certain air of triumph."

As other real names tumbled out, the oldest boys and girls began to comprehend that most of them were connected through the failed coup. Friewi later recalled how one of his housemates "had accidentally found out there were children named Stauffenberg among us, as well as children bearing other names of so-called 'traitors to the fatherland' who had been mentioned in the papers." He and the other young children did not fully grasp the implications of this discovery. The older ones, though, began to understand not just what connected them but why they had been brought together. They were being punished because of the actions of their fathers.

Christa refused to accept the idea that their families had been disgraced. "Would you never be allowed to say your name again?" she asked in her diary. "Were you really supposed to be ashamed of your origins forever? No, I could never do that; we must be proud of Father and of the others too!"

Then the children's situation seemed to change. In early October staffers began to notify them that they would be returning to their families. This unexpected development prompted Christa and Uta to quiz their house caretaker, Miss Köhne, about the circumstances behind their detentions. Christa recorded the woman's reply in her diary: "We were originally supposed to stay eight weeks in Sachsa. Our parents and older siblings were to have been killed during that time. Then the older children would have been sent to National Political Boarding Schools, and the little ones would have been given to SS families. They had taken our pictures away so that we 'would forget our first parents as quickly as possible!' "

The girls were stunned to discover what had previously been planned. Still, it made chilling sense. The confiscation of family keepsakes. The separation of siblings. The assignment of new names. All these steps would have made it easier to hide and divide the families permanently. When viewed within the context of Heinrich Himmler's original Sippenhaft plans, each action matched the Nazi objective of erasing the bloodlines of coup conspirators.

Some people now regard the children's new surnames as having been assigned at random. Others speculate that they may have corresponded to actual families that were waiting to adopt them. Few records exist about Sippenhaft, and it's not clear why the adoptions did not take place. Historians have pondered the possibilities. Perhaps the policy was relaxed because its initial severity was deemed sufficient to discourage any further uprising against the regime. Alternatively, as the breadth of the conspiracy became clear, Nazi leaders may have hesitated to fully enforce their plans because doing so would reveal the extent of the opposition they had faced.

After two months of persecution, 49 men had been executed for participating in the plot. Their family members had been arrested and detained in part to pressure the men to reveal the names of co-conspirators. Few had complied, and the leverage became irrelevant after their deaths. Executions continued, but many of the families were allowed to regroup.

In early October Gestapo agents returned to the Borntal to claim Wilhelm and his brother Christoph for a reunion with family members. Another escort took Friewi back to Ilse's home, where he was later reunited with his mother and older sister. And Uta and her sister, Heidi, departed to rejoin their mother near Berlin. Throughout that month 23 of the 44 children returned to their families.

But no one came for Christa or the rest of the residents. She and another 20 children remained in seclusion on the edge of Bad Sachsa, trapped in limbo and held against their will as pawns in a game of family punishment where few seemed to know the rules.

Or what move came next.

Adolf Hitler disembarks from an airplane with Joseph Goebbels (second from right) and other Nazi officials, circa 1944.

CHAPTER 6

Hitler's Demise

"[I]t is clear that there was no easing of National Socialist terror
against the German population in general,
but rather a constant expansion up to the end of the war."

Johannes Tuchel
Historian, 2017

By the late fall of 1944, Nazi officials had a Sippenhaft public
relations problem. Rumors about the policy were rampant,
and Joseph Goebbels was losing control of the story. He hadn't
reported that the Nazis were murdering the children of
Germany's elite families—nor were they—but that's the word
that was starting to spread through the officer corps of the
military and beyond. His press updates had not indicated that
the children's mothers were being killed—that wasn't happening either—but hearsay suggested otherwise. According to
these unfounded reports, the Valkyrie purge had become a
brutal bloodletting across genders and generations. In an effort
to squelch this erroneous speculation, the head of the regime's
security operations sent a letter in mid-December to his
Gestapo and surveillance agents asking them to promote a
corrective message.

German historian Johannes Tuchel has called the document "a masterpiece of political disinformation" because it is
so full of lies. Children weren't being killed, the memo

asserted, nor were they being permanently separated from family members. They were just receiving care while their mothers were temporarily held for questioning. The notice claimed that the changing of children's names—which had become controversial—was actually a caring maneuver designed to protect the youngsters from "unnecessary hostility from their surroundings." The memo's recipients were instructed to reassure the public that each child had been "returned to their respective mother as soon as she could be released from imprisonment."

But no such reunions were under way for the children left behind at the Borntal. Nor were they being planned for the more than 100 older relatives who continued to be detained. Some of these adults and teens remained in prisons. Others had been transferred to detention cells at concentration camps, including Nina von Stauffenberg, who was pregnant. Still others had been moved to a remote mountain inn. These detainees were ordered to conceal their identities and were kept under constant guard. Christa's mother and two older siblings were part of this group. So were members of the Goerdeler family and other von Stauffenbergs. "The thought automatically came up again and again," observed one of Carl Friedrich Goerdeler's daughters, Marianne Meyer-Krahmer: "Will they do something to us now that they have us all together?" Others felt uneasy too. One evening her 14-year-old sister Nina asked her: "Do you think they'll kill us tomorrow?"

Family members weren't held at the inn for long. From there they embarked on an almost endless sequence of moves that involved stays at concentration camps, including the notorious Buchenwald and Dachau sites. Sippenhaft detainees at these locations were isolated from the thousands of prisoners trapped in the Nazi's inhumane and often fatal system of forced labor, but they also faced exposure to deadly illnesses.

Berthold and his siblings lost a grandmother and great-uncle to malnutrition and typhoid fever in the camps.

Some of those who survived the endless detention began to speculate that they were being kept alive by Heinrich Himmler for use as bargaining chips after Germany lost the war. "Himmler had given precise orders that none of us must die," recalled a young woman named Fey von Hassell, whose father had been tied to the failed coup. She assumed that "Himmler must have hoped in this moment of collapse that his life would be spared by the Allied forces if he protected ours." She reasoned that Hitler had probably been told that all of them already had been killed, as he had ordered. The secrecy of their detention supported that lie, and their frequent moves allowed Himmler to prevent the ever encroaching Allied forces from liberating them.

As the months passed, a few other children were permitted to leave the Borntal, and by early February 1945 only 12 remained. These five boys and seven girls all were from families tied to the failed coup. By that point a new supervisor named Elsa Verch was caring for them, and everyone was living under one roof. The children had endured multiple seasons together, a bleak Christmas away from home, the contagion of childhood illnesses, and the relentless worries that accompanied their uncertain position.

One thing had changed: The war was getting closer. Air raid warnings had begun to sound at night during the late fall of 1944, sending everyone to the basement for shelter. Soon the alerts came during daylight hours too. But another thing remained constant: The children continued to be held against their will with no relief in sight.

"The likelihood that the Nazis would simply change their minds and still put us up for adoption into SS families seemed more real as weeks and months passed without any news from our families," Christa later noted. The family separations, the seclusion, the boredom, the uncertainty and unending anxiety—it all took its toll.

"I suffered a bit from the isolation," Berthold observed. "I'd read the newspaper every day before that. I liked to know what was going on." But all that ended after his transfer to the Borntal. There was "no contact at all."

Then, in February, two young brothers joined the group. They were introduced as random refugees with the last name of Hoffmann who had gotten separated from their family during transit. But within days Christa had carefully teased facts out of three-year-old Rainer and discovered that he and his 16-month-old brother were the grandsons of none other than Carl Friedrich Goerdeler, the man who had been slated to lead Germany after the coup. The boys' parents had been swept up with their grandfather and multiple other relatives after Valkyrie. Care for the children had fallen by default to a farm family that lived and worked on the parents' estate. One of Rainer's earliest childhood memories was being confined with the pigs as punishment when he cried. In November the

Rainer Goerdeler and his infant brother, Carl, 1944

brothers had been removed from the estate, but no records or childhood memories survive to account for where they were taken or why it took until February for them to reach Bad Sachsa.

That same month a team of German military officers and engineers took up residence in vacant buildings at the Borntal. These men were the brainpower behind a nearby secret rocket-making site. Enslaved laborers worked there around the clock to build an early missile called the V2 rocket. Hitler had hoped this so-called miracle weapon would improve Germany's chances in the war, but it failed to work in time. The captive children knew nothing about the work of their new neighbors, and the latest residents had no idea of the significance of the boys and girls they observed taking quiet strolls around their shared grounds. But each group watched the other with interest. The engineers speculated that the youngsters had been brought together because they were deaf, mistaking their improvised hand signals for actual sign language. In consequence they coined a nickname for the silent young walkers. They called them *Geisterkinder.*

Ghost children.

The morale of the girls and boys fluctuated between despair and hope as their detentions stretched from winter toward spring. "March 11, Father's birthday," became one of the occasions Christa documented in her diary. "It was another hard, sad day," she summarized after the anniversary. "I knew nothing of him, and the question of whether he was still alive tormented me especially on that day. That evening when I was alone, I wept many tears of homesickness and longing into my pillow."

And yet earlier that month she had observed the children's growing optimism. "Soon we had convinced ourselves that we had not been moved for so long because the idea of another [state-run] home for us had been absolutely abandoned, and they were now working on accelerating our journey home. It was not long before I believed quite firmly in this idea and envisaged its implementation more and more clearly and beautifully," Christa observed. "It was once again a case of waiting from day to day, from hour to hour."

Then, quite remarkably, the children were told that this long-awaited day was near. They would soon rejoin "our

The Borntal's infirmary building, late 1930s. It was the final residence for children detained at the property during Sippenhaft.

mothers and siblings—all our loved ones" in what staffers called "the 'other home,'" noted Christa. Spirits soared as the children celebrated Easter together and prepared to leave. In keeping with the strange contradictions of their confinement, the staff members who assured their detention also thoughtfully organized a special meal and an outdoor egg hunt to mark the holiday.

Two days later, on the afternoon of April 3, 1945, all the children and three of their caregivers climbed aboard a military transport truck and rushed to catch a train in nearby Nordhausen. Their vehicle left the Borntal about 30 minutes later than planned, a fact that almost undoubtedly saved their lives. For as they approached the city, the travelers heard the familiar wailing alert of an impending air raid. Their driver parked the group beneath some trees in a vain attempt to seek shelter.

And then the bombs began to fall.

"There was an insane buzzing, and suddenly a deafening banging and whistling set in," observed Christa. "The little children began to scream—we big ones lost all trace of color.

The fourteen of us lay tangled in a knot on the ground; the three adults accompanying us stared mutely at each other, with looks that meant to say—this is our last hour!" she wrote in her diary.

"It was really scary," recalled Berthold years later, "but somehow, I think, the smaller ones didn't realize how serious it was. They first told us that it was heavy antiaircraft fire." But the children were witnessing far more than antiaircraft fire. Bombs fell for an interminably long period of time, screeching through the air and shaking the ground when they struck. This attack and one the following day killed more than 8,000 people in the area.

There would be no family reunions for the children that day. No further trains could arrive or depart from the local rail station because the attack had destroyed it. Had the group reached the depot on time, they almost certainly would have been killed during the raid.

With all forward momentum blocked, their truck slowly wound its way out of town and through the surrounding countryside back toward Bad Sachsa. Christa witnessed the

Aftermath of air raids over Nordhausen, Germany, early April 1945. An estimated 75 percent of the city was destroyed during two days of bombing on April 3 and 4.

breadth of the devastation as they traveled. "I was already so shaken mentally by the hail of bombs in Nordhausen, where our lives seemed almost irretrievably clasped by death, that this desolate sight shook me terribly and despair threatened to overcome me." That night the children were right back where they had started, in their old beds at the Borntal.

What the children did not know at the time was that the bombing had rescued them from being delivered not just to any "other home," as their caregivers had described it, but to the Buchenwald concentration camp. This transfer had been designed to prevent them from being liberated by advancing Allied troops. But soldiers were approaching Buchenwald, too, so their relatives were likewise being relocated—an update that probably hadn't reached the Borntal staff. If the journey had gone as planned, the two groups could easily have missed one another.

Had the children completed their travels, German historian Johannes Tuchel has observed, they "would have been cast into the chaotic final days at Buchenwald before the camp's liberation on April 11, 1945." This circumstance, he noted, "could have been considerably more dangerous for them than staying in Bad Sachsa during the last days of the war." As the Allies approached Buchenwald, SS officers had forced their prisoners to evacuate, embarking on a march that led to many fatalities. The children could very easily have been swept up in that deadly confusion.

Back at the Borntal, staff members prepared for the inevitable arrival of Allied soldiers. The children began sleeping in their clothes and were not permitted to leave their residence. "Each of us kept a small case or a backpack with necessities at hand in case of an emergency," Christa noted in her diary. "Food was also packed, in case we had to flee to the forest at the last moment." Soon the children could hear cannons booming in the distance. Repeated air raid warnings sent everyone to the basement so often that they seemed to live belowground rather than above it.

On Sunday, April 8, the Allies bombed the community of Bad Sachsa itself. "All hell broke loose outside," Christa wrote. "There were rattles, whistles, bangs, buzzes, and whatever other noises are conceivable." Several thousand American troops reached the town four days later. In their effort to secure it, they began to scour the area for hostile forces, including at the Borntal. Because German military officers and their associates had left three days earlier, the property's transfer to Allied control was completed without a fight.

After years of wartime propaganda, many Germans eyed the arriving troops warily. "At the time," wrote Christa, "I never thought the Americans had liberated us; to me they were ghastly because they were the enemies of the Germans!"

When American soldiers realized that the Borntal served as a children's home, they left it alone. But as the end of the war neared, Allied officials became increasingly curious about its young residents. On at least two occasions they questioned the children about their backgrounds. During one session they asked them to reveal their real names. Willi Müller, whom the Allies had designated to serve as the new local mayor, began talking with the children too. During one of his visits, he delivered what Christa called "a solemn speech." The mayor proclaimed: "And now your names are the same as before. There's no need to be ashamed of your names or your fathers because they were heroes!" Christa felt like shouting and laughing for joy.

She wrote in her diary: "At last the time had come. Someone had come who understood me and who thought in exactly the same way as I did."

Even as Germany tumbled through chaos toward defeat, its Nazi machinery of control continued to whirl and hum. "The bureaucracy worked to the very end," Berthold later noted. Trials, imprisonments, and the killing of accused conspirators continued. The executioners hanged Carl Friedrich Goerdeler, young Rainer's grandfather, on February 2, 1945. Carl's brother, the boys' great-uncle Fritz, was murdered four weeks later. Friedrich Fromm had been branded a coward for failing to stop the coup and was shot on March 12. On April 9 SS guards executed a conspirator named Ludwig Gehre, whose daughter and stepdaughter were at the Borntal. His death made the girls orphans because their mother had died the previous fall in the midst of his capture. Georg Elser, who'd been imprisoned since 1939 for attempting to assassinate Hitler, was singled out for execution by the dictator and also died on April 9. Three weeks later Hitler took his own life. His regime collapsed soon after with Germany's surrender on May 7, 1945.

By the end of the war, families had been displaced all over Germany, and many communities lay in ruins. A few conspirators actually outlived the regime. Some survived in secret hiding places. Others managed to acquire forged identity

Sketch by a Stauffenberg family member of the Sippenhaft detention area at Buchenwald concentration camp, 1945

papers and slip out of the country. A few even escaped detection altogether. American soldiers finally caught up with the group of older Sippenhaft captives at a hotel in the Italian Alps. It took time to figure out who they were, whether or not they had been tied to the regime, and if they should be released. Some of them waited months before they were finally allowed to return to their homes.

Thank-you note from Sippenhaft prisoners to a local baker, April 1945. The baker had supplied food to the group while it was waylaid in his town.

In the meantime, relatives who were already free began to seek their missing children. Among those searching was Alexandrine Gräfin von Üxküll-Gyllenband. She was a countess as well as a great-aunt of the Stauffenberg and Hofacker children. Known to them variously as Aunt Üllas or Aunt Lasli, she had been detained like other Stauffenberg relations during Sippenhaft. But she had won early release within weeks because of her critical war work as director of the Red Cross in Germany.

When the war ended, Aunt Lasli used her connections to search for her missing nieces and nephews. For example, she sent a request to Catholic authorities in Rome: Could they help the family find its children? Her query became one of the Vatican's missing person radio bulletins broadcast across Europe after combat ceased. Someone from Bad Sachsa apparently heard the request for information about existing clusters of parentless minors and reported, as Christa later put it: "There was a bunch of children living in a home at the forest and nobody knows who they are." This tip helped lead Aunt Lasli to her young relations.

On June 11, 1945, as Christa later wrote, "the day came that had been the focus of my longing and hoping—of all of my thoughts." They were found. It had been no small task for Aunt Lasli to travel across the war-ravaged country. Many bridges, roads, and railways had been damaged or destroyed. Passage through the territory was carefully controlled by Allied forces, each of which had been given one of four zones to manage. Aunt Lasli's importance with the Red Cross helped her gain the required permits from Allied administrations for a cross-country journey of hundreds of miles. A French officer even loaned her a vehicle for the trip, which was a tremendous help at a time when cars and fuel were in short supply.

When Aunt Lasli reached the Borntal, she discovered not only the six Stauffenberg cousins, but her three Hofacker relations too. She took responsibility for transporting all of them home along with a fellow resident named Marie-Luise Lindemann. Because she could not fit so many people in one

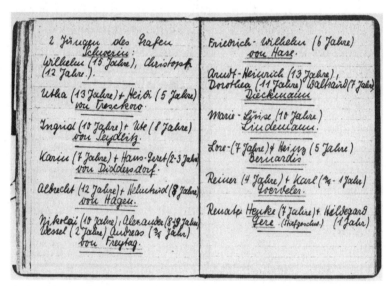

A partial listing of the children held with Christa von Hofacker at the Borntal as noted in her diary

vehicle, the ever resourceful woman hired a local bus for the return trip, one that had the advantage of being equipped with an oven that converted wood into gas fuel.

Four children remained after this group departed: Rainer Goerdeler, his younger brother, and the orphaned half sisters Renate Henke and Hildegard Gehre. The mother of the Goerdeler boys reached them in late July. It was November before Mayor Müller and the Borntal's Elsa Verch could track down relatives to claim the sisters. By then Müller and Verch had fallen in love; they married soon after.

Christa had learned the fate of her father when Aunt Lasli arrived. After enduring months of uncertainty, her worst fears were

Alexandrine Gräfin von Üxküll-Gyllenband, 1954. She was also known as both Aunt Lasli and Aunt Üllas.

confirmed: Cäsar von Hofacker was dead. He had been executed shortly before Christmas. As Christa prepared to depart the place where she'd spent nearly 10 months of confinement, this news swirled with the rest of the day's revelations. "In bed that evening, I lay awake a long time, with my thoughts revolving around one thing: Father is dead—but the others are alive—this is the last night in Sachsa—

"We're free!"

Workers install a light over the headless statue of an SS guard at the entrance to a former Nazi barracks, Berlin, March 13, 1947. American soldiers beheaded the statue after taking control of the area. The rest of the figure and other monuments to the regime were removed during a postwar period of denazification.

CHAPTER 7

A Traumatic Shadow

"And now all this is two years ago, and we're living in Krottenmühl again, almost unchanged. Or does it only seem unchanged to the observer? Has a deep wound not been inflicted on our lives, one that is only slowly healing?"

Christa von Hofacker, age 14
Diary entry, Christmas, 1946

Ghost children. When German engineers created this nickname, they had no notion how apt a label it really was. They had noticed the silence in which the girls and boys walked on the Borntal's grounds, but they couldn't have realized that the children's inner lives had become muffled too. The trauma of family separation and the uncertainty of their situation had left their marks.

Because of Sippenhaft, the children who emerged from the Borntal were not the same people they had been before. And the homes they returned to were not the homes they had left behind. Not only were most of their fathers gone, "the total destruction and chaos that surrounded us, brought new challenges," Christa observed years later. Mothers struggled to provide for their families as single parents. "You had to have food, you had to have clothes, you had to have wood that you collected from the forest to heat your ovens," Christa recalled. "We had no money. We had no home. We had nothing. We started with less, rather than from scratch."

Indeed, the whole country was starting with less than scratch. City centers, houses of worship, schools, and other institutions of society had almost invariably been damaged by physical destruction, or the warped ideology of the regime, or both. When the boys and girls returned to school after leaving the Borntal, they discovered that the slandered reputations of their fathers accompanied them. "Some children pointed their fingers at me and suddenly didn't want to be in my company anymore," noted Albrecht.

"We were treated as traitors," Friewi observed, because that's what schoolchildren were initially taught to believe about the children's fathers. "We had to grow up with this. And so it was, for a young boy, very hard, because I knew that he had acted to save Germany."

Girls and boys, seated separately by gender, share copies of their text in a classroom in postwar Germany, undated.

Nazi ideology had been spread so widely and had soaked in so deeply that a decade or more passed before Germany's citizens recognized what the mayor of Bad Sachsa had seen immediately: that the fathers behind the coup had been heroes. Even in the 1950s the teachers of Rainer Goerdeler characterized participants in the German resistance movement as traitors. He later observed: "[H]ere it became obvious that Hitler's 'seeds' had taken root in the heads of the people far beyond the existence of the Third Reich!"

It took decades to retrain or replace educators steeped in Nazi ideology and to produce lessons and textbooks that acknowledged the valor of the resistance and the atrocities of the regime, including Nazi concentration camps and the Holocaust. The generation of children born after the war came to realize that many of their teachers and family members had been unwilling or unable to present an honest accounting of the country's recent history. In 1968, young adults mounted street protests to demand that Germans be taught the truth about the Nazi regime. Such actions prompted additional reforms and a more public acknowledgment of past mistakes.

But the change was not universal. After the war Germany was divided into two separate countries, each with its own distinct political beliefs and educational systems. Eastern regions fell under control of the communist-based Soviet Union, while the rest formed a democratically led government that aligned itself with Western Europe and the United States. This division endured for 41 years until Germany reunited as a single democracy in 1990. The study and interpretation of the nation's past took on fresh urgency after reunification and continues to this day.

The children who had once been held captive on the edge of Bad Sachsa grew up, went to universities, married, became parents, and welcomed grandchildren into their lives. But

Gottliebe Gräfin von Lehndorff-Steinort with her daughters (from left), Marie Eleonore (Nona), Gabriele, Catharina, and Vera, 1949, five years after their husband and father had been killed for being a Valkyrie conspirator

many of them, even as adults, could not shake the specters that had begun to shadow them during Sippenhaft. "My experience of the events connected with 20 July and its aftermath were so traumatic," Friewi recalled, "that for a long time I was both unwilling and unable to talk, let alone write about it. And the burden of the past was difficult to carry for other members of my family, too." Years later, in an act that proved therapeutic, he collected and edited personal accounts from his own family and others into a compelling portrayal of what he titled *Hitlers Rache,* or Hitler's revenge.

Friewi's sister Maria-Gisela has described how the shock of her father's death and the cruelty of his execution left her feeling "frozen" for decades. "I was just, you go through the day and so on and nothing is of importance anymore. And I think it was for years that I had that feeling of emptiness."

Each Sippenhaft survivor has similarly struggled to make peace with the past. Some have been able to forgive their parents' choices more easily than others. Christa came to see her father's actions as an effort to right a wrong, after having initially supported the regime. "When he realized his error, he joined the resistance." But every person naturally had their own individual response. The one thing that united all of them was the shared experience with trauma. Christa came to believe that "no one throughout Europe who survived the war came away without the scars of suffering deep losses. Everyone lost loved ones, friends, homes, belongings."

Uta von Tresckow (left) and Christa von Hofacker, 1948. The girls developed a lifelong friendship.

●·············●·············●·············●·············●

After the war the Allies worked to hold Germany accountable for its crimes, and many people were punished. But the Nazi regime's offenses were so widespread and its accomplices so numerous that not nearly all of them were identified, charged, or disciplined. Some notorious figures hadn't survived the war. Roland Freisler, the infamous judge, died in early 1945 when an Allied bomb made a direct hit on his People's Court. In

Ilse-Lotte von Hofacker (far left) with her children in Tutzing, Germany, 1949. Back row, from left: Alfred and Eberhard. Front row, from left: Christa, Liselotte, and Anna-Luise.

The courtroom scene in Nuremberg, Germany, where trials for the most notorious Nazi war criminals took place, November 24, 1945. All but three of the 22 defendants were found guilty by an international military tribunal. Twelve were sentenced to death by hanging.

addition to Hitler, several other key figures committed suicide before they could be punished, including Joseph Goebbels, the propaganda minister, and Heinrich Himmler, the long-standing SS leader and home defense minister who had directed Sippenhaft.

Hundreds of Nazi leaders and deputies were brought before judges at postwar trials in Nuremberg, Germany, and elsewhere during subsequent years. Given the regime's multiple crimes against humanity, it may not be surprising that few people were scrutinized for their ties to the enforcement of Sippenhaft. So many actions had taken place that were far crueler and more deadly. The lack of surviving records about the policy made it easier to overlook too.

Not only did the criminality of family punishment escape any meaningful notice; the entire Sippenhaft story nearly dropped from the historical record. "Our fate is not something extraordinary in the picture of the war," Christa later observed, recognizing that the post-Valkyrie crackdown pales in comparison to World War II's larger atrocities. "People suffered so much worse. People suffered in every which way. They lost children, they lost homes, they lost husbands, it's unimaginable. So our fate was not extraordinary."

It took the reunification of Germany and the passage of 50 years before local and national historians became interested in what had happened to the children confined outside of Bad

The Borntal's House 3, November 2, 2018. Children facing long-term Sippenhaft detentions spent the winter months here before being relocated in the spring of 1945 to the infirmary building. The old house sits unused and abandoned today.

Sachsa. Only then did they begin to interview the survivors and present their stories to the general public. This work helped foster greater awareness of the breadth and depth of German resistance to the Nazi regime. It also provided a fuller understanding of the scope and intensity with which Hitler ruthlessly sought to maintain his dictatorial control. Eventually federal and local governments would mount major exhibitions about the history and host commemorations attended by surviving family members, the German chancellor, and other dignitaries.

Over time Christa's diary became famous in her home country. It serves as a rare primary source document from an almost forgotten segment of Hitler's regime. Christa's record exists in part because after the war she wanted to answer her

Title page from the diary that 14-year-old Christa von Hofacker gave to her mother in 1946. She copied her original notes into a bound volume, "Unsere Zeit in Sachsa," or "Our Time in Sachsa." The accompanying text translates as, "A detailed diary of the past year/by Christa/for Mommy/Christmas 1946/ The most difficult year 1944–45/For Mommy, in memory of our long separation/ Christa/(1944: 12 years old)."

mother's persistent question: *What happened?* "I lost a year with all of you," she would say. "You talk about it all the time, but it's not the same." So in 1946 Christa converted her personal notes into a narrative as a gift for her mother. She later observed, "It would have never occurred to me, that my little diary is now quoted time and again and considered an important document of its time. When I wrote it as a Christmas present for my mother, it was simply an attempt to catch her up with the year of our childhood that was lost to her."

In 1998 Bad Sachsa town leaders organized the first local reunion of the people who had been held as children on the outskirts of the community. Christa and Berthold had each visited the site as adults, but few others had ever returned. Most had never before met as adults or even seen one another after they'd departed the Borntal five decades earlier. Despite the passage of time, their tour of the site stirred long-forgotten memories.

Many wandered silently around the property, lost in thought, ghost children once again.

Angela Merkel, chancellor of Germany, speaks to Sippenhaft survivors, their families, other dignitaries, and guests during the 75th commemoration of the Valkyrie coup attempt, July 20, 2019. Such gatherings occur annually in the Bendler Block courtyard.

"Seventy-five years after the failed coup
we commemorate the men and women of
the 20th of July 1944 with the greatest of respect.
They acted when others were silent.
They followed their conscience. They took responsibility for
their and our country when others looked away.
They faced up to an inhumane system.
They were very aware what consequences their action might
have for themselves and their families.
They were willing to make the greatest of sacrifices.
Their lives."

German Chancellor Angela Merkel
commemorating the attempted Valkyrie coup
Berlin, July 20, 2019

Timeline

This timeline includes key events from the rise to power of Adolf Hitler, World War II, the Valkyrie coup attempt, and the related Sippenhaft family punishment.

November 11, 1918
Germany's surrender at the conclusion of the First World War and the subsequent Treaty of Versailles lead to such punishing terms of defeat that it becomes difficult for the country to regain its stability.

November 9, 1923
Adolf Hitler and supporters in Munich attempt to seize control of Bavaria, one of the states of Germany. The effort collapses within hours. During the nine-month imprisonment that follows, Hitler writes *Mein Kampf (My Struggle),* a book detailing his life story and political vision that helps fuel his subsequent rise to power.

October 29, 1929
New York City financial markets collapse, triggering the beginning of what becomes known as the Great Depression. The worldwide economic hardships that follow become an important factor in Hitler's political rise to power.

July 1932
Hitler's National Socialist German Workers' (Nazi) Party wins nationwide elections, positioning him to be appointed chancellor of Germany months later on January 30, 1933.

June 30, 1934
During what becomes known as the Night of the Long Knives, Hitler initiates a massive purge of political enemies and eliminates the paramilitary SA leadership. This campaign helps him consolidate his control over the state security apparatus.

August 2, 1934
When Germany's president, Paul von Hindenburg, dies, Hitler merges the duties of the vacant office with his role as chancellor and becomes the nation's dictator. The head of the armed forces orders all service members to swear their allegiance to Hitler.

1936–38
Hitler begins to regain control over territory that was once part of Germany, including the Rhine region near France, Austria, and a section of Czechoslovakia. International leaders tolerate his moves in order to avoid war, so Hitler makes plans for further expansion.

November 9–10, 1938
During what becomes known as Kristallnacht, or Night of Broken Glass, the Gestapo mounts a nationwide attack against Jewish

people, businesses, and houses of worship. Many German citizens aid in the theft and destruction of Jewish property, including 1,500 synagogues and prayer rooms. Further persecutions follow, setting the stage for the subsequent mass detention and murder of millions of Jews and other marginalized peoples at Nazi death camps during the Holocaust.

March 15, 1939
In violation of the Munich Agreement, which is an update of the Treaty of Versailles, Hitler orders German forces to occupy all remaining Czech territory.

September 1, 1939
Germany invades Poland, prompting declarations of war from Great Britain and France. World War II begins. The Soviet Union joins the fight 16 days later when it invades Poland too.

November 8, 1939
In an attempt to kill Adolf Hitler, a carpenter named Georg Elser plants a bomb in a Munich beer hall set to explode during an annual speech. Hitler unexpectedly cuts his remarks short and is not there when the timed device detonates later.

April 9, 1940
German armed forces invade Denmark and Norway.

May 10, 1940
Germany launches an invasion of western European countries that quickly spreads through the Netherlands, Luxembourg, Belgium, and France, vastly expanding the territory under Hitler's control and alarming the international community.

June 22, 1941
Despite an existing signed agreement with Joseph Stalin that the two dictators would not attack each other, Hitler sends German forces into the Soviet Union, opening up an eastern front of combat in World War II.

December 8, 1941
The United States declares war on Japan after the previous day's attack by Japanese bombers on Pearl Harbor in Hawaii. Within days the United States is at war with Germany and its fighting partner Italy.

1942–43
In 1942 British forces land on the African continent and begin to push German forces from the northern territories it has claimed there. American forces join the effort the next year. Claus Schenk Graf von Stauffenberg is gravely injured during combat in Tunisia on April 7, 1943. By the next month German forces have been defeated in Africa.

1943–45

American and British troops advance from North Africa to Italy and laboriously reclaim the country from fascist Italian and German forces. Italian dictator Benito Mussolini is overthrown on July 25, 1943. Although initially imprisoned, the former dictator is freed by German soldiers and taken to Germany.

June 6, 1944

Gen. Dwight D. Eisenhower coordinates the landing of Allied troops on the Normandy beaches in France, and forces begin to liberate the country as they march east toward the Rhine region of Germany.

July 20, 1944

Stauffenberg attempts to kill Hitler during a meeting at the Wolfsschanze, or Wolf's Lair. The attempt fails along with a related military coup code-named Valkyrie.

July 30, 1944

Hitler meets with Field Marshal Wilhelm Keitel, the chief of Germany's armed forces, and Heinrich Himmler, the country's home defense minister, to formalize the Nazi response to the Valkyrie attacks. They institute Sippenhaft, or family punishment for relatives of the accused.

July–August 1944

Gestapo agents begin rounding up suspects in the failed plot as well as their relatives, including children and infants. Most teens and adults are sent to prison, where they are questioned and held indefinitely. Younger children are almost all transported to Bad Sachsa in central Germany, where they are held at a nearby state facility for young people, the Borntal. Coup participants appear before a show court; almost all are executed in the hours or weeks that follow.

September–October 1944

Some adults and teens are released from prison and reunited with their younger family members. Other adults and children remain under arrest for the duration of the war, either at various concentration camps, other sites, or at the Borntal.

April 3, 1945

An attempt is made to transfer the last of the children from the Borntal to Buchenwald concentration camp, but an Allied bombing of the Nordhausen rail station prevents this move.

April 12, 1945

American forces reach Bad Sachsa and assume command over the area, including the children still being held at the Borntal.

April 16, 1945

The Soviet military begins its assault on Berlin. By April 25 its forces have surrounded the capital city. Hitler takes shelter belowground in a military command bunker.

April 30, 1945

Hitler commits suicide in his underground bunker in Berlin, ending his 12-year reign over Germany. Berlin falls under Soviet control two days later, and fighting stops in the capital city.

May 4, 1945

Newly appointed Bad Sachsa mayor Willi Müller takes charge of the children being detained nearby and urges them to be proud of their fathers' actions in the Valkyrie coup attempt.

May 7, 1945

Germany surrenders, bringing an end to the nearly six-year-long war in Europe. World War II continues in the Pacific until Japan surrenders on August 14, 1945.

June 11, 1945

Alexandrine Gräfin von Üxküll-Gyllenband (who was called both Aunt Üllas and Aunt Lasli) reaches the Borntal.

July 27, 1945

The Goerdeler boys are reunited with their mother after she comes to claim them at the Borntal.

November 1945

Half sisters Hildegard Gehre and Renate Henke leave Bad Sachsa, the last of the detained children to do so. Their parents had been killed during Sippenhaft, so their care falls to an uncle on the German island of Föhr.

May 23, 1949

Germany is formally divided in two. The western territory becomes the Federal Republic of Germany. The eastern portion falls within the bloc of Soviet Union countries and is called the German Democratic Republic. Berlin is likewise divided. The regions do not reunite until 1990, following the fall of the Berlin Wall.

July 20, 1952

Family members take part in the first commemoration of the 1944 events at the Bendler Block courtyard where four Valkyrie conspirators were executed after the coup's collapse. Over time the actions of Stauffenberg and his associates come to be viewed as heroic, not traitorous. The street in front of the Bendler Block is renamed in Stauffenberg's honor in 1955. Permanent exhibitions about the coup attempt and other acts of Nazi-era German resistance open in a neighboring building during 1989.

The Borntal's Sippenhaft Families

After the failed Valkyrie coup, 46 children from 19 families were held for weeks or months at the Borntal on the edge of Bad Sachsa during 1944–45. The following list outlines these families' circumstances under Sippenhaft. It does not include the many other families whose members were detained, punished, and killed after Valkyrie on the orders of Adolf Hitler.

KEY

Names are presented as they were known in 1944–45 and do not reflect subsequent changes due to marriage, etc.

Boldface indicates parents who were executed, committed suicide, or otherwise died because of Sippenhaft and the attempted coup.

★ indicates people arrested and detained during Sippenhaft, but who survived.

Italics indicate children who were interned at the Borntal. Ages shown are approximate as of arrival.

Bold italics indicate children who were detained until after the end of World War II.

TERMS FOR GERMAN HEREDITARY TITLES

Freiherr = Baron
Freifrau (Baronin) = Baroness
Graf = Count
Gräfin = Countess

BERNARDIS

Pronunciation: Bear-NAR-dis
Father: **Robert Bernardis**
Mother: Hermine Bernardis★
Children:
Lore (daughter, age six)
Heinz (son, age four)
Other relatives detained: yes

DIECKMANN

Pronunciation: DEEK-munn
Father: **Wilhelm Dieckmann**
Mother: Erika Dieckmann★
Children:
Barbara (daughter, age 16)★
Arend-Heinrich (son, age 13)
Dorothea (daughter, age 11)
Waltraut (daughter, age seven)
Other relatives detained: yes

DITTER VON DITTERSDORF

Pronunciation: DITT-er fonn DITT-ers-dorf
Father: Bruno Ditter von Dittersdorf (previously deceased; not involved in Valkyrie plot)
Mother: Ingeborg Ditter von Dittersdorf★
Children:
Karin (daughter, age five)
Hans-Gerret (son, age three)
Other relatives detained: none

FREYTAG VON LORINGHOVEN

Pronunciation: FRY-tag fonn LOH-ring-hof-en
Father: **Wessel Freiherr Freytag von Loringhoven**
Mother: Elisabeth Freifrau Freytag von Loringhoven★
Children:
Nicolai (son, age nine)

Axel (son, age eight)
Wessel (son, age two)
Andreas (son, age one)
Other relatives detained: yes

GEHRE & HENKE
Pronunciation: GERE-ra & HEN-ka
Father: **Ludwig Gehre**
Mother: **Hanna Gehre**
(formerly Henke)
Children:
Renate Henke (stepdaughter of
Ludwig, age five)
Hildegard Gehre
(daughter, age 19 months)
Other relatives detained: yes

GOERDELER
Pronunciation: GIR-de-ler
Grandfather: **Carl Friedrich**
Goerdeler
Father: Ulrich Goerdeler★
Mother: Irma Goerdeler★
Children:
Rainer Johannes Christian
(son, age three)
Carl (son, age 16 months)
Other relatives detained: yes

HAGEN
Pronunciation: HAA-gen
Father: **Albrecht von Hagen**
Mother: Erica von Hagen★
Children:
Albrecht (son, age 11)
Helmtrud (daughter, age eight)
Other relatives detained: yes

HANSEN
Pronunciation: HUN-sen
Father: **Georg Alexander Hansen**
Mother: Irene Hansen★
Children:
Hans-Georg (son, age 11)
Wolfgang (son, age eight)
Karsten (son, age six)
Frauke (daughter, age two)

Dagmar (daughter, age one month)
Other relatives detained: none known

HASE
Pronunciation: HAA-ze
Father: **Paul von Hase**
Mother: Margarethe von Hase★
Children:
Baronin Ina von Medem
(daughter, age 21, née von Hase)
Maria-Gisela (daughter, age 20)★
Alexander (son, age 19)★
Friedrich-Wilhelm
("Friewi"; son, age seven)
Other relatives detained: yes

HAYESSEN
Pronunciation: HIGH-yes-sen
Father: **Egbert Hayessen**
Mother: Margarete Hayessen★
Children:
Hans-Hayo (son, age two)
Volker (son, age nine months)
Other relatives detained: yes

HENKE (see GEHRE)

HOFACKER
Pronunciation: HOHF-auck-er
Father: **Cäsar von Hofacker**
Mother: Ilse-Lotte von Hofacker★
Children:
Eberhard (son, age 16)★
Anna-Luise (daughter, age 14)★
Christa (daughter, age 12)
Alfred (son, age nine)
Liselotte (daughter, age six)
Other relatives detained: yes

LEHNDORFF-STEINORT
Pronunciation:
LEHN-dorf–SHTYN-ort
Father: **Heinrich Graf von**
Lehndorff-Steinort
Mother: Gottliebe Gräfin von
Lehndorff-Steinort★

Children:
Marie Eleonore ("Nona"; daughter, age six)
Vera (daughter, age five)
Gabriele (daughter, age 20 months)
Catharina (daughter, born during detention in August 1944)★
Other relatives detained: yes

LINDEMANN
Pronunciation: LYNN-de-munn
Father: **Fritz Lindemann**
Mother: Lina Lindemann★
Children:
Friedrich (son, age 21)★
Georg (son, age 19)★
Marie-Luise (daughter, age 10)
Other relatives detained: none known

SCHWERIN VON SCHWANENFELD
Pronunciation: Shverr-EEN fonn SHVAAN-en-felt
Father: **Ulrich-Wilhelm Graf von Schwerin von Schwanenfeld**
Mother: Marianne Gräfin von Schwerin von Schwanenfeld★
Children:
Wilhelm (son, age 15)
Christoph (son, age 11)
Detlef (son, age nine weeks)★
Other relatives detained: yes

SEYDLITZ
Pronunciation: SIDE-lits
Father: Walther von Seydlitz (not involved in Valkyrie plot)
Mother: Ingeborg von Seydlitz★
Children:
Ingrid (daughter, age 10)
Ute (daughter, age eight)
Other relatives detained: yes

STAUFFENBERG
Pronunciation: SHTOW-fen-bearg
Father: **Berthold Schenk Graf von Stauffenberg**
Mother: Maria (Mika) Schenk Gräfin von Stauffenberg★
Children:
Alfred (son, age six)
Elisabeth (daughter, age five)
Other relatives detained: yes (two died during captivity)

STAUFFENBERG
Pronunciation: SHTOW-fen-bearg
Father: **Claus Schenk Graf von Stauffenberg**
Mother: Nina Schenk Gräfin von Stauffenberg★
Children:
Berthold (son, age 10)
Heimeran (son, age eight)
Franz-Ludwig (son, age six)
Valerie (daughter, age three)
Konstanze (daughter, born during detention in 1945)★
Other relatives detained: yes (two died during captivity)

TRESCKOW
Pronunciation: TRES-co
Father: **Henning von Tresckow**
Mother: Erika von Tresckow★
Children:
Mark (son, soldier, age 16)— killed at the front
Rüdiger (son, sailor, age 15)
Uta (daughter, age 13)
Adelheid ("Heidi"; daughter, age four)
Other relatives detained: none known

TROTT ZU SOLZ
Pronunciation: TROT tsue SOLL-ts
Father: **Adam von Trott zu Solz**
Mother: Clarita von Trott zu Solz★
Children:
Anna-Verena (daughter, age two)
Clarita (daughter, age nine months)
Other relatives detained: none known

Resource Guide

FURTHER READING

Bartoletti, Susan Campbell. *Hitler Youth: Growing Up in Hitler's Shadow.* Scholastic Nonfiction, 2005.

Freedman, Russell. *We Will Not Be Silent: The White Rose Student Resistance Movement That Defied Hitler.* Clarion Books, 2016.

Giblin, James Cross. *The Life and Death of Adolf Hitler.* Clarion Books, 2002.

Hendrix, John. *The Faithful Spy: Dietrich Bonhoeffer and the Plot to Kill Hitler* (graphic biography). Amulet Books, Abrams, 2018.

Hoose, Phillip. *The Boys Who Challenged Hitler: Knud Pedersen and the Churchill Club.* Farrar, Straus and Giroux, 2015.

Wilson, Kip. *White Rose* (historical fiction in verse). Versify, Houghton Mifflin Harcourt, 2019.

DOCUMENTARY FILMS

Heller, André, and Othmar Schmiderer, dirs. *Blind Spot: Hitler's Secretary.* Dor Film Produktionsgesellschaft, 2002. German-language interviews with Traudl Junge, Hitler's secretary, with English subtitles. Rated PG.

Ze'evi, Chanoch, dir. *Hitler's Children.* Maya Productions, 2011. German, English, and Hebrew with English subtitles. Unrated.

PLACES TO VISIT IN PERSON AND ONLINE

Bad Sachsa Museum of Local History (Heimatmuseum Bad Sachsa)
Hindenburgstraße 6
37441 Bad Sachsa, Germany
Phone (from U.S.A.):
   +49-5523-999436
"'Our True Identity Was to Be Destroyed.' The Children Consigned to Bad Sachsa After July 20, 1944" (exhibit)

German Resistance Memorial Center (Gedenkstätte Deutscher Widerstand)
Stauffenbergstraße 13-14
10785 Berlin-Mitte, Germany
Phone (from U.S.A.):
   +49-30-269950-00
gdw-berlin.de/en/home/

National World War II Museum
945 Magazine St.
New Orleans, LA 70130
Phone: 504-528-1944
nationalww2museum.org/

Plötzensee Memorial Center (Gedenkstätte Plötzensee)
Hüttigpfad
13627 Berlin-Charlottenburg-Wilmersdorf, Germany
gedenkstaette-ploetzensee.de/index_e.html

Topography of Terror Documentation Center (Dokumentationszentrum Topographie des Terrors)
Niederkirchnerstraße 8
10963 Berlin, Germany
Phone (from U.S.A.):
   +49-30-254509-50
topographie.de/

United States Holocaust Memorial Museum
100 Raoul Wallenberg Pl., SW
Washington, DC 20024-2126
Phone: 202-488-0400
ushmm.org/
USHMM Holocaust Encyclopedia
encyclopedia.ushmm.org/en

A sign welcoming visitors at the Bad Sachsa train station, November 2, 2018. When the Hofacker children disembarked at the station in 1944, they had to walk two miles to reach the Borntal because of wartime transportation scarcities.

A Note From the Author

People keep diaries for all sorts of reasons. They allow us to preserve the everyday, capture treasured memories, and ponder the turning points of our lives. They give voice to our concerns by transforming tangled thoughts into words. They help us make sense of the present, and they remind us *you were there* in a way that allows us to reflect on how, over time, *you have arrived here.*

The entries in Christa von Hofacker's diary are a record of her experiences during the closing months of the Nazi regime, but they also commemorate her passage through the innocence of childhood to the edge of adulthood. She was a resourceful but frightened adolescent when she reached the Borntal. By the time she emerged after 10 months of detention, she had become a resilient and independent young woman. When I became acquainted with Christa seven decades later, she demonstrated the same determined spirit and confidence that had carried her through what she characterized in her diary as "the most difficult year" of 1944–45— and through all the years that followed.

I consider my long-distance friendship with Christa to be one of the greatest gifts of my writing career. So was the privilege of exploring her story and those of the other 45 former young residents of the Borntal. After 20 years of writing books for children, I finally had the chance to write one about them. Even though I met or spoke with Christa and several other Sippenhaft survivors when they were silver-haired adults, at my desk she and the others always materialized as fully formed seven-, 10-, and 12-year-olds. The details of this book are taken from months of research and the hundreds of note cards I'd meticulously filled with facts.

But its heart comes from these children, and I am grateful.

Research Notes
and Acknowledgments

I'm not sure who got more excited in 2015 when my oldest son and I set off from Berlin one brisk January morning on a quest to visit the Wolf's Lair. We departed aboard a sleek express train and spent the day transferring to a series of ever simpler rail carriages until, by twilight, we finally reached an outpost in Poland named Ketrzyn (roughly pronounced KETCH-in). The next morning snowflakes began to fall as we set out off for the former Nazi bunker. Our guided rambles around the frozen ruins of this site remain one of the most otherworldly explorations I've ever made.

Three years later Sam and I returned to Europe for further research. This time we homed in on the events of Valkyrie and what followed. We stood in the courtyard at the Bendler Block in Berlin where Claus von Stauffenberg and others had been shot, found our way to the execution chamber of Plötzensee Prison, and made a pilgrimage to Bad Sachsa. Together we walked the grounds of the Borntal, studied the vacant houses where the Nazis had confined their captured children, and, with permission, explored the abandoned corridors and living spaces inside one of them.

Many individuals helped make these travels more productive and pleasant, including Beate and Helmut Heseker, who hosted us and arranged for our private tour of the site of the SS headquarters in Wewelsburg; Czeslaw Puciato, our guide through the vast and tangled complex of abandoned bunkers and associated structures at the Wolf's Lair; and Ralph Boehm, the local historian who introduced us to the Bad Sachsa region and shared his vast knowledge about the children who had once been confined nearby.

Staff members at the German Resistance Memorial Center, especially historians Petra Behrens and Johannes Tuchel, provided crucial scholarship and support for this project. So did Melanie Frey at the July 20, 1944, Foundation, who shared an English translation of Christa's diary with me and introduced me to key Sippenhaft survivors. I owe extra thanks to Dr. Behrens, Mrs. Frey, Lutz Ackermann, family members, and others who supplied invaluable images (see illustration credits).

My accounting of this history would have been sorely diminished without the conversations I had with Maria-Gisela von Hase Boehringer, Friedrich-Wilhelm (Friewi) von Hase, Christa von Hofacker Miller, and Berthold Schenk Graf von Stauffenberg. It was my privilege and joy to interview all four of these eyewitnesses to history, either by phone or in person. Transcribing our lengthy conversations was a monumental task, and I am grateful to my younger son, Jake, for his patient labors with this work. I also appreciate the transcription help

The author and Professor Friedrich-Wilhelm (Friewi) von Hase at his home in Germany, November 5, 2018

Memorial to Claus von Stauffenberg and other members of the German resistance at the bombing site where the Valkyrie coup attempt began, Wolf's Lair, Poland, January 20, 2015

and other assistance offered by Lauren Rachel Woolf, who worked with me as a Beloit College student intern during the closing months of my research.

Professor von Hase further aided my work through his collection of Sippenhaft remembrances in the volume *Hitlers Rache* (Hitler's revenge). His book awaits translation into English, but in the meantime I gained access to key sections of it thanks to Christoph Bausum, one of my delightful German cousins and someone who, in a happy coincidence, works as a professional translator. I'm grateful to Christoph for his invaluable work and to our fellow cousin Jacob and his wife, Claudia, who generously hosted Sam and me during our travels.

My father—who had used his skills as an historian to reconnect our long-separated family strands in 1965—was still alive when I started this book, but he died at age 94 near the conclusion of my research. He remains a steadying influence on my work nonetheless, as do my mother, to whom he was married for 71 years, my brother and his wife, my sons, of course, and countless friends. I'm grateful for the early manuscript feedback I received from critique group partners Georgia Beaverson, Pam Beres, Judy Bryan, and Jamie A. Swenson, and for the review of other outside readers. These include historian, author, and professor Peter Hoffmann, whose books about the von Stauffenberg family and the German resistance aided my research immeasurably; Michal Hoschander Malen, children's and YA editor at the Jewish Book Council; Christoph Bausum; and Christa von Hofacker Miller.

Memorial statue in the courtyard of the Bendler Block, October 30, 2018. This commemorative bronze casting of a bound figure was unveiled on July 20, 1953, nine years after the failed coup.

This project marks the fourth time I've benefited from the freelance editorial wizardry of Catherine Frank. May the trend continue. It is my first pairing with in-house editor Ariane Szu-Tu at National Geographic Partners—and, I hope, not the last. Additionally I'm indebted to past and present members of the publisher's talented team of editorial, production, and marketing associates, including Eva Absher-Schantz, Becky Baines, Ruth Chamblee, Tammi Colleary-Loach, Julide Dengel, Jennifer Emmett, Lori Epstein, Joan Gossett, Kate Hale, Laurie Hembree, Anne LeongSon, Vivian Suchman, Gus Tello, Ruth Thompson, and Andi Wollitz. There would be no book without them.

Our efforts are a salute to the spirit of perseverance— among writers, among editors, among readers, and among those whose stories we share, including the ghost children.

Citations

The following names have been abbreviated: Maria-Gisela Boehringer (née von Hase) (MGB); Friedrich-Wilhelm (Friewi) von Hase (FWH); Christa von Hofacker Miller (CHM); Wilhelm Graf von Schwerin von Schwanenfeld (WSS); and Berthold Schenk Graf von Stauffenberg (son of Claus) (BSS).

Opening Quote
9 Claus von Stauffenberg: "It is now time … traitor to his own conscience." (Hoffmann, *German Resistance to Hitler,* 135).

Introduction
10 Anne Frank: "I'm finally getting optimistic … has been made on Hitler's life." (Frank, 205).

Chapter 1: Hitler's Rise
13 Victor Klemperer: "Words can be like tiny doses … sets in after all" (Klemperer, 14); **16** Fritz Gerlich: "Adolf Hitler is preaching … wake up!" (Ullrich, 641); **17** Victor Klemperer: "Some kind of fog has descended which is enveloping everybody" (Klemperer, 34); **17** Poster: "Führer, we're following you!" (Steur and Kutzner, 28); **20** German military oath of allegiance: "unconditional obedience" and "to risk my life at any time for this oath" (Holocaust Encyclopedia, online); **22** Cäsar von Hofacker: "do away with elections once and for all" (Hoffmann, *Stauffenberg,* 59); **24** FWH: "It was very impressive … Nothing else. Only this" (Hase, author interview); **25** BSS: "Of course I believed … becoming a little Nazi" (Stauffenberg, *Auf einmal ein Verräterkind,* 11; reprinted in and translated from Hase, *Hitlers Rache,* 81); **25** Victor Klemperer: "Nazism permeated the flesh and blood … mechanically and unconsciously" (Klemperer, 14); **25** BSS: "one realized, if only vaguely … feeling of subtle threat" (Stauffenberg, *Auf einmal ein Verräterkind,* 14; reprinted in and translated from Hase, *Hitlers Rache,* 83); **26** WSS: "Opposition was not welcome … penalties and extra drills." (Schwerin, 143).

Chapter 2: Resisting the Regime
29 Carl Friedrich Goerdeler: "The German people must and will … and freedom of the German people" (Gedenkstätte Deutscher Widerstand website); **30** Carl Friedrich Goerdeler: "Hitlerism is poison for the German soul" (Hoffmann, *The History of the German Resistance,* 58); **36** Philipp Freiherr von Boeselager: "Our primary role … and returned home" (Boeselager, 125); **38** White Rose leaflet: "a dictatorship of evil" ("The White Rose"); **39–40** CHM: "it was carpeted with bombs … and we never went back" (Miller, author telephone interview, October 19, 2018); **42** CS: "The men are wetting their pants or have sawdust in their heads" (Steinbach and Stiepani, 49).

Chapter 3: Valkyrie

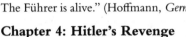

45 Berthold Schenk Graf von Stauffenberg (brother of Claus): "The most terrible thing ... and our children" (Steinbach and Stiepani, 98); **47** Philipp Freiherr von Boeselager: "We knew our roles by heart ... remain compartmentalized" (Boeselager, 153); **49** Henning von Tresckow: "The coup must still be attempted ... nothing else matters" (Steinbach and Stiepani, 78); **51** Margarethe von Hase: "Finally he told me that there were plans to assassinate Hitler" (Hase, *Hitlers Rache,* 23); **56** Erich Fellgiebel: "Something fearful has happened. The Führer is alive." (Hoffmann, *German Resistance to Hitler,* 122).

Chapter 4: Hitler's Revenge

61 Adolf Hitler: "I speak to you ... forged a plot to eliminate me" (Gisevius, 212); **62** Adolf Hitler: "I have been saved ... to the end." (Heller and Schmiderer); **62** Adolf Hitler: "I myself am wholly unhurt," "are now being mercilessly exterminated" (Gisevius, 212); **63** BSS: "the führer was at least ... outside our imagination" (Stauffenberg, author interview); **63** Peter Hoffmann: "voicing so monstrous a suspicion against such a distinguished officer" (Hoffmann: *The History of the German Resistance,* 410); **65** Adolf Hitler: "small clique" (Gisevius, 212); **66** MGB: "Without saying goodbye, it was farewell forever" (Hase, *Hitlers Rache,* 35); **68** Adolf Hitler: "They must have no time for speeches!" (Hoffmann, *German Resistance to Hitler,* 134); **68** Baronin Ina von Medem (née von Hase): "In a few hours, Papi will no longer be with us" (Behrens and Tuchel, 92); **68** Heinrich Graf von Lehndorff-Steinort: "My most beloved in the world!" (Vollmer, 341; reprinted in and translated from Hase, *Hitlers Rache,* 124); **68** Heinrich Graf von Lehndorff-Steinort: "I am unhappy ... It's all just love and love again" (Vollmer, 350; reprinted in and translated from Hase, *Hitlers Rache,* 133); **70** Sippenhaft policy, November 21, 1944: "spouse, children, siblings, parents, and other relatives" (Tuchel, 159); **71** Heinrich Himmler: "You need only to read ... a cad and a traitor." (Tuchel, 154); **72** Joseph Goebbels: "creating extraordinary domestic unrest" (Tuchel, 154); **72** Albrecht von Hagen: "without any hint ... at the manor house at the time" (Hase, *Hitlers Rache,* 114); **73** Baronin Ina von Medem: "What will happen ... A family has been wiped out" (Behrens and Tuchel, 92); **75** Margarethe von Hase: "Every night women from the other cells were taken to their executions" (Hase, *Hitlers Rache,* 27); **75** Margarethe von Hase: "he told me that I, too ... verse for this last journey" (Hase, *Hitlers Rache,* 28); **75** MGB: "'The first days are the worst,' but I don't think that's true." (Hase, *Hitlers Rache,* 36); **75** Prison inmate: "Don't cry girl, your father's dead." (Hase, *Hitlers Rache,* 38); **75** MGB: "must have cut out this specific article and passed it on to me" (Hase, *Hitlers Rache,* 41); **76–77** MGB: "When my mother and I came out ... and said, 'What now?' " (Boehringer, author telephone interview, October 26, 2018).

Chapter 5: The Ghost Children

79 CHM: "[On August 24] that dreadful Gestapo man ... he made them come true" (Hofacker, 8); **80** BSS: "there were hate-filled ... in the newspapers every day." (Stauffenberg, *Auf einmal ein Verräterkind,* 17; reprinted in and translated from Hase, *Hitlers Rache,* 85); **80** BSS: "The housekeeper took us ... courageous these words were" (Stauffenberg, *Auf einmal ein Verräterkind,* 18; reprinted in and translated from Hase, *Hitlers Rache,* 85); **84** CHM: "Three caretakers appeared ... We were separated" (Hofacker, 14-15); **85** CHM: "he was in terrible despair ... bravely swallowing his tears" (Hofacker, 17-18); **85** CHM: "She didn't let anybody touch ... staring straight ahead" (Miller, author telephone interview, October 19, 2018); **86** CHM: "These first few days were terrible ... why this suffering?' " (Hofacker, 18); **87–88** WSS: "Life in the home ... on how to behave" (Schwerin von Schwanenfeld, 146); **88** FWH: "There are some ... better than others" (Hase, author interview); **88** FWH: "knowing nothing about their fate was a heavy burden" (Hase, *Hitlers Rache,* 63); **88** CHM: "Thinking of Father ... bravely in the eye" (Hofacker, 24); **88** Uta von Tresckow: "Listen, Christa ... and yours probably is too!" (Hofacker, 19); **88** CHM: "simultaneously broke the bolts ... feeling suddenly light" (Hofacker, 19); **88–89** FWH: "but that his real name ... with a certain air of triumph" (Hase, *Hitlers Rache,* 61-62); **89** FWH: "had accidentally found out ... mentioned in the papers" (Hase, *Hitlers Rache,* 62); **90** CHM: "Would you never be allowed ... proud of Father and of the others too!" (Hofacker, 34); **90** CHM: "We were originally ... as quickly as possible!' " (Hofacker, 27).

Chapter 6: Hitler's Demise

93 Johannes Tuchel: "[I]t is clear that there was no easing ... the end of the war" (Tuchel, 171); **93** Johannes Tuchel: "a masterpiece of political disinformation" (Tuchel, 172); **94** Nazi memo, December 14, 1944: "unnecessary hostility from their surroundings" (Tuchel, 172); **94** Nazi memo, December 14, 1944: "returned to their respective ... released from imprisonment." (Tuchel, 172); **94** Marianne Meyer-Krahmer (née Goerdeler): "The thought automatically ... have us all together?" (Behrens and Tuchel, 123); **94** Nina Goerdeler: "Do you think they'll kill us tomorrow?" (Behrens and Tuchel, 123); **95** Fey von Hassell: "Himmler had given ... if he protected ours" (Hassell, page unidentified; reprinted in and translated from Hase, *Hitlers Rache,* 152); **95–96** CHM: "The likelihood that the Nazis ... news from our families" (Miller, correspondence with the author, March 5, 2019); **96** BSS: "I suffered a bit ... no contact at all" (Stauffenberg, author interview); **97** CHM: "March 11, Father's birthday ... into my pillow" (Hofacker, 64); **97** CHM: "Soon we had convinced ... from hour to hour" (Hofacker, 63-64); **97–98** CHM: "our mothers and siblings—all our loved ones" and "the 'other home' " (Hofacker, 67); **98–99** CHM: "There was an insane buzzing ... this is our last hour!" (Hofacker, 69); **99** BSS: "It was really scary ... antiaircraft fire." (Stauffenberg, author interview); **100** CHM: "I was already so shaken ... threatened to overcome me" (Hofacker, 72); **100** Borntal staff members: "other home" (Hofacker, 67); **100** Johannes Tuchel: "would have been cast ... last days of the war." (Tuchel, 170); **100** CHM: "Each of us kept ... at the last moment." (Hofacker, 74); **101** CHM: "All hell broke loose ... other noises are conceivable." (Hofacker, 74); **101** CHM: "At the time ... enemies of the Germans!" (Hofacker, 76); **101** CHM: "a solemn speech" (Hofacker, 78); **101** Willi Müller: "And now your names are the same ... they were heroes!" (Hofacker, 79); **101** CHM: "At last the time had come ... same way as I did" (Hofacker, 79); **102** BSS: "The bureaucracy worked to the very end" (Stauffenberg, author interview); **103** CHM: "There was a bunch of children ... nobody knows who they are" (Miller, author telephone interview, October 19, 2018); **104** CHM: "the day came ... of all of my thoughts" (Hofacker, 82); **105** CHM: "In bed that evening ... We're free!" (Hofacker, 83-84).

Chapter 7: A Traumatic Shadow

107 CHM: "And now all this is two years ago ... only slowly healing?" (Hofacker, 86); **107** CHM: "the total destruction and chaos that surrounded us, brought new challenges" (Miller, correspondence with the author, March 12, 2019); **107** CHM: "You had to have food ... rather than from scratch" (Miller, author telephone interview, October 19, 2018); **108** Albrecht von Hagen: "Some children pointed ... in my company anymore" (Hase, *Hitlers Rache,* 117); **108** FWH: "We were treated as traitors" (Hase, author interview); **108** FWH: "We had to grow up ... he had acted to save Germany" (Hase, correspondence with the author); **109** Rainer Johannes Christian Goerdeler: "[H]ere it became obvious ... the Third Reich!" (Hase, *Hitlers Rache,* 143); **110** FWH: "My experience of the events ... of my family, too." (Hasse, *Hitlers Rache,* 67); **110** MGB: "frozen" and "I was just ... feeling of emptiness" (Boehringer, author telephone interview); **111** CHM: "When he realized his error, he joined the resistance" (Miller, author telephone interview, October 19, 2018); **111** CHM: "no one throughout Europe. ... loved ones, friends, homes, belongings" (Miller, correspondence with the author February 4, 2020); **113** CHM: "Our fate is not ... our fate was not extraordinary" (Miller, author telephone interview, October 19, 2018); **114** CHM: "Our Time in Sachsa... 12 years old" (Hofacker, 1); **115** Ilse-Lotte von Hofacker: "I lost a year ... it's not the same." (Miller, author telephone interview, October 19, 2018); **115** CHM: "It would have never occurred ... lost to her." (Miller, correspondence with the author, March 12, 2019).

Closing Quote

117 Angela Merkel: "Seventy-five years after the failed coup ... Their lives." (Merkel).

A Note From the Author

127 CHM: "the most difficult year" (Hofacker, subtitle of diary).

Bibliography

Books

Boeselager, Philipp Freiherr von. *Valkyrie: The Story of the Plot to Kill Hitler, by Its Last Member,* Trans. 2009 Weidenfeld & Nicolson. Vintage Books, 2010.

Frank, Anne. *Anne Frank: The Collected Works.* Bloomsbury Continuum, 2019.

Gisevius, Hans Bernd. *Valkyrie: An Insider's Account of the Plot to Kill Hitler.* Da Capo Press, 2009.

Hase, Friedrich-Wilhelm von. *Hitlers Rache: Das Stauffenberg-Attentat und seine Folgen für die Familien der Verschwörer* [Hitler's revenge: The Stauffenberg assassination attempt and its consequences for the conspirators' families]. SCM Hänssler, 2014. Excerpts translated from the German by Christoph Bausum.

Hassell, Fey von. *Storia incredibile.* Bescia, Italy: Editrice Morcelliana, 1987.

Hoffmann, Peter. *German Resistance to Hitler.* Harvard University Press, 1988.

———. *The History of the German Resistance, 1933-1945,* 3rd ed., Trans. Richard Barry. McGill-Queen's University Press, 1996.

———. *Stauffenberg: A Family History, 1905-1944,* 3rd ed., Trans. by the author. McGill-Queen's University Press, 2008.

Klemperer, Victor. *The Language of the Third Reich: A Philologist's Notebook,* Trans. Martin Brady. The Athlone Press, 2000; Continuum, 2006 (paperback). (Original German edition, LTI—*Lingua Tertii Imperii,* published 1947.)

Loeffel, Robert. *Family Punishment in Nazi Germany: Sippenhaft, Terror and Myth.* Palgrave Macmillan, 2012.

Mommsen, Hans. *Alternatives to Hitler: German Resistance Under the Third Reich,* Trans. Angus McGeoch. Princeton University Press, 2003.

Ohler, Norman. *Blitzed: Drugs in the Third Reich,* Trans. Shaun Whiteside. Houghton Mifflin Harcourt, Mariner Books, 2018.

Riedesel, Valerie Freifrau zu Eisenbach. *Geisterkinder: Fünf Geschwister in Himmlers Sippenhaft* [Ghost children: five siblings in Himmler's family detention]. SCM Hänssler, 2017.

Schulthess, Konstanze von. *Nina Schenk Gräfin von Stauffenberg: Ein Porträt.* Piper Verlag, 2008.

Stauffenberg, Berthold Schenk Graf von. *Auf einmal ein Verräterkind* (Stuttgarter Stauffenberg-Gedächtnisvorlesung, Bd. 2011). Göttingen, Germany: Wallstein Verlag, 2012.

Ullrich, Volker. *Hitler: Ascent 1889–1939,* Trans. Jefferson Chase. Alfred A. Knopf, 2016.

Vollmer, Antje. *Doppelleben. Heinrich und Gottliebe con Lehndorff im Widerstand gegen Hitler und von Ribbentrop.* Berlin: Aufbau Verlag, Die Andere Bibliothek, 2010, 2011.

Museums, Catalogs, and Online Resources

Behrens, Petra, and Johannes Tuchel. *"Our True Identity Was to Be Destroyed":* *The Children Consigned to Bad Sachsa After July 20, 1944,* Trans. Katy Derbyshire. Gedenkstätte Deutscher Widerstand (German Resistance Memorial Center), 2017.

Dokumentationszentrum Topographie des Terrors (Topography of Terror Documentation Center), Berlin, Germany. topographie.de.

Gedenkstätte Deutscher Widerstand (German Resistance Memorial Center), Berlin, Germany. gdw-berlin.de/en/home.

Gedenkstätte Wewelsburg 1933–1945 (Wewelsburg 1933–1945 Memorial Museum), Wewelsburg, Germany. wewelsburg.de/en/gedenkstaette-1933-1945.

Puciato, Czesław. *Wolfsschanze: Hitler's Headquarters in East Prussia, a Guide* (English edition). Bartograf (book publishing service), 1997.

Steinbach, Peter, and Ute Stiepani. *Claus Schenk Graf von Stauffenberg and the Attempted Coup of July 20, 1944,* dual-language ed., Trans. Katy Derbyshire. Gedenkstätte Deutscher Widerstand (German Resistance Memorial Center), 2008.

Steur, Claudia, and Mirjam Kutzner. *Berlin 1933–1945: Between Propaganda and Terror,* Trans. Karen Margolis. Stiftung Topographie des Terrors (Topography of Terror Foundation), 2010.

Topography of Terror—Gestapo, SS, and Reich Security Main Office on Wilhelm- and Prinz-Albrecht-Straße: A Documentation, Trans. Pamela Selwyn et al. Stiftung Topographie des Terrors (Topography of Terror Foundation), 2010.

United States Holocaust Memorial Museum, Washington, D.C., ushmm.org; Holocaust Encyclopedia, encyclopedia.ushmm.org/en.

"The White Rose" (exhibition catalog), Trans. Katy Derbyshire. Gedenkstätte Deutscher Widerstand (German Resistance Memorial Center), 2015.

Primary Source Documentation

Boehringer, Maria-Gisela (née von Hase). Author telephone interview (in English), October 26, 2018.

———. Author telephone interview (in English), July 13, 2019.

Hase, Friedrich-Wilhelm von. Author interview (in English), Mannheim, Germany, November 5, 2018.

———. Correspondence with the author, October 18, 2019.

Heller, André, and Othmar Schmiderer, dirs. *Blind Spot: Hitler's Secretary* (documentary film). Dor Film Produktionsgesellschaft, 2002.

Hofacker, Christa von. "Our Time in Sachsa: A Detailed Diary of the Past Year, The Most Difficult Year, 1944-45" (previously translated as "Our Time in Sachsa: A Detailed Diary of the Past Year, The Hard Year, 1944-45") ["Unsere Zeit in Sachsa: Ein Ausfuhrliches Tagebuch des Vergangenen Jahres, Das Schwere Jahr, 1944-45"], Trans. Gedenkstätte Deutscher Widerstand (German Resistance Memorial Center). Unpublished manuscript, December 1946.

A wall of remembrance dedicated to more than 200 Valkyrie conspirators at the German Resistance Memorial Center in Berlin, October 2018. Most lost their lives in punishment after the plot failed.

Merkel, Angela. "Merkel Speech at 75th Anniversary of Hitler Assassination Attempt." Deutsche Welle, DW News (video with dubbed English translation), https://www.youtube.com/watch?v=ZhBPCLiIc3o.

Miller, Christa (née von Hofacker). Author telephone interview (in English), October 19, 2018.

———. Author telephone interview (in English), September 17, 2019.

———. Correspondence with the author, February 28, 2019.

———. Correspondence with the author, March 5, 2019.

———. Correspondence with the author, March 12, 2019.

———. Correspondence with the author, February 4, 2020.

Schwerin von Schwanenfeld, Wilhelm Graf von. "Speech for the Opening of the Exhibition 'Our True Identity Was to Be Destroyed'." Bad Sachsa, Germany, November 22, 2016. Reprinted in *"Our True Identity Was to Be Destroyed": The Children Consigned to Bad Sachsa After July 20, 1944,* by Petra Behrens and Johannes Tuchel, Trans. Katy Derbyshire. Gedenkstätte Deutscher Widerstand (German Resistance Memorial Center), 2017.

Stauffenberg, Berthold Schenk Graf von. Author interview (in English), Oppenweiler, Germany, November 6, 2018.

Stauffenberg, Marie-Gabriele Schenk Gräfin von. *Aufzeichnungen aus unserer Sippenhaft 20. July 1944 bis 19. Juni 1945.* Stuttgart, Germany: Haus der Geschichte, undated.

Scholarly Research and News Media Articles

Baldwin, Hanson W. "Hitler 'Lair' Opened to Tourists." *New York Times,* June 9, 1962.

Beckert, Helen. "The Effects of Denazification on Education in West Germany." Honors thesis, Murray State University, 2016. https://digitalcommons.murraystate.edu/scholarsweek/2016/GermanHistory/4.

Carey, Benedict. "Can We Inherit Trauma?" *New York Times,* December 11, 2018.

Case, J. David. "The Politics of Memorial Representation: The Controversy Over the German Resistance Museum in 1994." *German Politics and Society* (Spring 1998). https://www.jstor.org/stable/23737408.

Eddy, Melissa. "They Resisted Hitler and Were Executed. Finally, They Are Laid to Rest." *New York Times,* May 14, 2019.

Edelman, Hope. "No Quick Fix for Childhood Grief." *New York Times,* August 26, 2019.

Hochschild, Adam. "The Eleventh Hour." *New Yorker,* November 5, 2018.

Hodapp, Martin. "Germany's Rocket Development in World War II." *Hohonu* (2013). https://hilo.hawaii.edu/campuscenter/hohonu/volumes/documents/GermanysRocketDevelopmentinWorldWarIIMartinHodapp.pdf.

Lyman, Rick. "After Years in the Shadows, Europe's Neo-Fascists Are Stepping Back Out." *New York Times,* March 20, 2017.

Neo, Hui Min, " 'They Were Denied a Grave': Microscopic Remains of Nazi Victims Given Final Resting Place." *The Local,* May 13, 2019. https://www.thelocal.de/20190513/they-were-denied-a-grave-microscopic-remains-of-nazi-victims-given-final-resting-place.

Smale, Alison. "A Burden of Nazism Grows Bigger With Time." *New York Times,* November 3, 2015.

Tuchel, Johannes. "The Reich Security Main Office 'Special Commission on July 20, 1944' and the Children's Consignment to Bad Sachsa," 2017. Reprinted in *"Our True Identity Was to Be Destroyed": The Children Consigned to Bad Sachsa After July 20, 1944,* by Petra Behrens and Johannes Tuchel, Trans. Katy Derbyshire. Gedenkstätte Deutscher Widerstand (German Resistance Memorial Center), 2017.

Text Permissions

See Bibliography and Citations for additional information.

Index

140

Illustration Credits

Published by National Geographic Partners, LLC.

Copyright © 2021 Ann Bausum. All rights reserved. Reproduction of the whole or any part of the contents without written permission from the publisher is prohibited.

NATIONAL GEOGRAPHIC and Yellow Border Design are trademarks of the National Geographic Society, used under license.

Since 1888, the National Geographic Society has funded more than 12,000 research, exploration, and preservation projects around the world. The Society receives funds from National Geographic Partners, LLC, funded in part by your purchase. A portion of the proceeds from this book supports this vital work. To learn more, visit natgeo.com/info.

For more information, visit nationalgeographic.com, call 1-877-873-6846, or write to the following address:

National Geographic Partners
1145 17th Street N.W.
Washington, DC 20036-4688 U.S.A.

The text permissions for this book appear on page 139.

For librarians and teachers: nationalgeographic .com/books/librarians-and-educators

More for kids from National Geographic: natgeokids.com

National Geographic Kids magazine inspires children to explore their world with fun yet educational articles on animals, science, nature, and more. Using fresh storytelling and amazing photography, *Nat Geo Kids* shows kids ages 6 to 14 the fascinating truth about the world— and why they should care. kids.nationalgeographic.com/subscribe

For rights or permissions inquiries, please contact National Geographic Books Subsidiary Rights: bookrights@natgeo.com

Jacket designed by Julide Dengel
Interior designed by Julide Dengel
and Ruthie Thompson

Hardcover ISBN: 978-1-4263-3854-0
Reinforced library binding ISBN:
978-1-4263-3855-7

Printed in U.S.A.
20/WOR/1